THE MOUNTAINS OF RONDA
AND GRAZALEMA

About the Author

Guy Hunter-Watts has lived and worked in Andalucía since the 1980s. After studying at the universities of Santiago and Salamanca he taught English in South America before moving to the Ronda mountains where he's been leading guided walks for almost 25 years. His work as a walking guide and freelance journalist has taken him to many corners of the planet including India, Namibia, Tanzania, Latin America and Mongolia.

Other Cicerone guides by the author
Coastal Walks in Andalucia
Walking in Andalucia

THE MOUNTAINS OF RONDA AND GRAZALEMA

by Guy Hunter-Watts

JUNIPER HOUSE, MURLEY MOSS,
OXENHOLME ROAD, KENDAL, CUMBRIA LA9 7RL
www.cicerone.co.uk

Printed by KHL Printing, Singapore
A catalogue record for this book is available from the British Library.
All photographs are by the author unless otherwise stated.

Route mapping by Lovell Johns www.lovelljohns.com
Contains OpenStreetMap.org data © OpenStreetMap
contributors, CC-BY-SA. NASA relief data courtesy

Updates to this Guide

While every effort is made by our authors to ensure the accuracy of guide-books as they go to print, changes can occur during the lifetime of an edition. Any updates that we know of for this guide will be on the Cicerone website (www.cicerone.co.uk/892/updates), so please check before planning your trip. We also advise that you check information about such things as transport, accommodation and shops locally. Even rights of way can be altered over time.

The route maps in this guide are derived from publicly available data, databases and crowd-sourced data. As such they have not been through the detailed checking procedures that would generally be applied to a published map from an official mapping agency, although naturally we have reviewed them closely in the light of local knowledge as part of the preparation of this guide.

We are always grateful for information about any discrepancies between a guidebook and the facts on the ground, sent by email to updates@cicerone.co.uk or by post to Cicerone, Juniper House, Murley Moss, Oxenholme Road, Kendal LA9 7RL, United Kingdom.

Register your book: To sign up to receive free updates, special offers and GPX files where available, register your book at www.cicerone.co.uk.

Front cover: Looking south to the Embalse de Zahara and the Sierra del Pinar from the summit of Lagarín (Walk 27)

CONTENTS

Acknowledgements

Having the help of volunteers at my home in Montecorto during the time I was compiling this guide was a huge help. Many thanks to Sarah Fox, Rafa Lopes, Aurélie Vesco, Daria Filmonova and Katarina Kostorova.

And an extra special thank you to Ola Leszczyńska for your help and company when I was researching routes in the Valle del Genal and the Sierra de las Nieves.

Symbols used on route maps

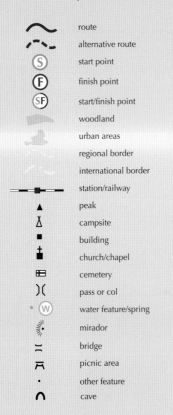

～	route
╴╴╴	alternative route
Ⓢ	start point
Ⓕ	finish point
⑤Ⓕ	start/finish point
	woodland
	urban areas
	regional border
	international border
▬■▬	station/railway
▲	peak
⋇	campsite
■	building
✚	church/chapel
⊞	cemetery
)(	pass or col
Ⓦ	water feature/spring
⋇	mirador
⊐⊏	bridge
⊼	picnic area
·	other feature
⌒	cave

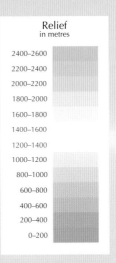

Relief
in metres

2400–2600	
2200–2400	
2000–2200	
1800–2000	
1600–1800	
1400–1600	
1200–1400	
1000–1200	
800–1000	
600–800	
400–600	
200–400	
0–200	

SCALE: 1:50,000

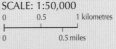

0   0.5   1 kilometres

0   0.5 miles

Contour lines are drawn
at 25m intervals and
highlighted at 100m
intervals.

GPX files

GPX files for all routes can be downloaded free at www.cicerone.co.uk/892/GPX.

Breach in the rocks on the way to the Lígar plateau (Walk 30)

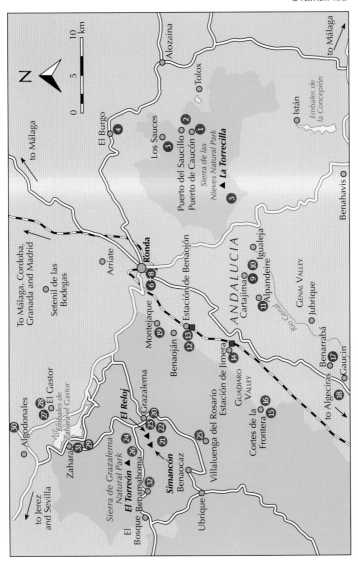

9

Bennarabá in the lower Genal valley (Walk 17)

AUTHOR'S PREFACE

I first visited Ronda in the mid-80s. Arriving when the Semana Santa processions were in full swing I soon fell under the spell of the town and its extraordinary physical surroundings.

In those days there were few waymarked trails in the area but the paths I was able to discover were of great beauty, and they inspired me to search out more. Some years later I returned, this time to buy an abandoned village house in one of the quietest of *los Pueblos Blancos* (the White Villages). It was there I struck up a friendship with Andrés Duarte, a kindly shepherd, who would later show me many of the old drovers' paths he'd known since his childhood. With Andrés as my guide I came to know the surrounding mountains far better and with each new trail discovered, my attachment for the region grew.

My time in the Ronda mountains has coincided with a new interest among both Spaniards and foreigners for rural tourism and, along with it, walking. Trails are now waymarked: three GR routes cross the area while many PR trails have been created linking the villages of both the Sierra de Grazalema and the Sierra de las Nieves, along with those of the Guadiaro and Genal valleys. Even though many companies now offer group and self-guided walking holidays in the area, you can rest assured that you'll meet with few other walkers and may even have the trail all to yourself.

Guy Hunter-Watts
2017

The path up towards Puerto de Cuco (Walk 2)

INTRODUCTION

Ronda seen from the ridge leading to the chapel of La Virgen de la Cabeza (Walk 7)

People's first associations of southern Spain are often of sun, sand and sea, of beachside resorts and tourism of the packaged variety. Yet this coastal belt, cradled to the east by the Mediterranean and to the west by the Atlantic, constitutes a tiny part of Andalucía, Spain's southernmost and most diverse autonomous region. Just a few kilometres inland from the sea the mighty Penibetic mountains rise steeply upwards, stretching like a vast sabre across southern Spain. From the high peaks of the Sierra Nevada – they rise to almost 3500m and are snow clad for several months of the year – this majestic chain gradually decreases in height before merging with the more northern Subbetic chain as they run west towards the Atlantic. These grandiose mountain ranges are home to some of the finest walking trails in Europe.

The market town of Ronda, the largest of *los Pueblos Blancos* (the White Villages), is cradled between two of the region's most beautiful Natural Parks: the Sierra de las Nieves to the east and the Sierra de Grazalema to the west. Both areas boast UNESCO biosphere status thanks not only to their great natural beauty but also to the diversity of their wildlife and plants.

The spectacular mountain passes and peaks surrounding Ronda, and the villages nearby, have attracted travellers to the region since the advent during the mid-19th century of what we now call tourism. The Romantic movement ensured that Ronda, along with Sevilla and Granada, became an essential part of the Grand Tour, nurturing a vision of Andalucía and its mountains as a land of bullfighters, bandoleros, flamenco and gypsies. Engravings, watercolours and paintings from the early Victorian era, typified by the work of David Roberts, helped spread the fame of the town whose stunning physical setting inspired many artists and writers and later attracted a flow of illustrious visitors. Mérimée's *Carmen* (set in Seville), later set to music in Bizet's opera, gilded a much romanticised Andalucían lily.

Today the town remains very much on the traveller's trail even though most visitors are daytrippers who arrive on organised coach excursions from the Costa del Sol. By mid-afternoon the crowds have departed and Ronda regains its dignity; this is the time to explore its labyrinthine old town centre, one of Europe's most beautiful historic quarters with views that are second to none.

Ronda was always the main market town for the villages of the surrounding mountains and until the advent of motorised transport an intricate network of footpaths saw the constant passage of villagers with their mules and donkeys, bringing goods to and from the town as well as buying and selling their animals at regular livestock markets. The footpaths were maintained by royal decree, from which the name *cañada real* or royal way is derived. Later, when these same goods began to be transported by lorry, passage along these ancient byways rapidly declined and local councils ceased to maintain the paths. The advent of walking tourism has changed all that and there is now a growing awareness that these same footpaths can bring welcome income to the villages that they connect.

Taking advantage of the European Community's CEDER programme for rural development, time and money have been invested in waymarking

Summer landscape south of Ronda (Walk 1)

local footpaths, some of which date back to Roman and Arab times. This initiative, hand in hand with the creation of the Natural Parks of the Sierra de las Nieves to the east and the Sierra de Grazalema to the west, means that the Ronda mountains now offer some of the finest hiking trails in Andalucía with a corresponding infrastructure of both hotels and restaurants.

The section that follows gives a brief overview of the three regions covered in this guide while a more detailed description is given at the beginning of each regional section.

THE THREE REGIONS

From east to west, the three regions covered by this guide are:

Ronda and the Sierra de las Nieves

Of the three areas described within this guide the Natural Park of the Sierra de las Nieves is the least well known yet it is home to one of the most grandiose expanses of mountains in southern Spain. Several of the park's peaks are more than 1500m while La Torrecilla at 1919m is the highest point in western Andalucía.

As the name implies, the mountains are often snowcapped in winter when they make a breathtaking backdrop to Ronda when seen from the west.

Wooded valleys and mountainsides, with the world's largest stands of Spanish fir (*Abiss pinsapo*), contrast with craggy outcrops of limestone

above the tree line, and there's a well-maintained network of hiking trails which cut into the heart of the Sierra from both its eastern and western sides.

Although you first need to drive along forestry tracks to reach most trailheads, this extra effort is richly rewarded and the drive to and from the walks can be an adventure in its own right.

In recognition of the unique beauty of the park, already a UNESCO biosphere reserve, within the coming year the area is due to be upgraded from 'Natural' to 'National' Park. The added kudos is bound to attract more visitors and more investment to the area.

This section also includes two delightful walks straight out from Ronda as well as one historical walk through the town's enchanting Moorish quarter which will lead you past all of its most emblematic monuments.

The Guadiaro and Genal valleys

Stretching south from Ronda the valleys of the Genal and Guadiaro rivers are home to some of Spain's most beautiful small villages.

The upper part of the Genal valley feels more remote and can only be accessed by one narrow, snaking road. Most walks here lead you through the valley's chestnut forests while those further to the south, in the area close to Gaucín, lead you through ancient stands of gall and holm oak.

15

The Guadiaro valley is more easily accessed from Ronda by both road and train, along the line that was built by the British at the end of the 19th century. You'll find some of the most stunning karst limestone scenery in Europe along with a string of delightful Pueblos Blancos, most of which have small hotels and several restaurants.

The Sierra de Grazalema

Stretching west from Ronda towards the Atlantic coast the Grazalema Natural Park offers some of the finest hiking on the Iberian peninsula. Fertile river valleys contrast with rugged peaks of limestone while ancient groves of almonds and olives alternate with forests of cork and gall oaks. The region's unusually wet climate helps explain the richly diverse plant life of the park, and to be here during the Andalucían springtime is an experience never to be forgotten.

Two of Spain's most beautiful mountain villages, Grazalema and Zahara de la Sierra, are both popular bases for walking holidays while a number of companies offer village to village tours that generally lead eastwards across the park to Ronda.

PLANTS AND WILDLIFE

Two major highlights of any walk in southern Spain come in the form of the flowers and birds you see along the way. Appendix E includes details of guidebooks that will help you to

*Hoop petticoat narcissus,
N.bulbocodium; borage, Borago
officinalis, a common sight
in the Ronda mountains*

identify the plants and wildlife of the region.

Birds

The mountains of Ronda and Grazalema number among the finest birding destinations in Europe and ornithological tourism has grown rapidly in recent years. The best time for birdwatching is during the spring and autumn migrations between Europe and North Africa, but at any time of year you can expect rich birdlife. For further information about birding resources and organised birding tours and walks, see Appendix B.

As well as seasonal visitors there are more than 250 species present throughout the year. If you'd like a list of the more common species visit www.cicerone.co.uk/803/resources. Several species of eagle nest within the park, and you're guaranteed sightings on nearly all walks in this area of soaring griffon vultures (*Gyps fulvus*) – sometimes a hundred or more – which nest in the deep gorges on the western side of the Grazalema Park.

Plants

The mountains and valleys around Ronda and Grazalema also offer rich rewards for botanists. Forty per cent of all species found in Iberia are present in Andalucía and many of these are to be found within these mountains, including a number of endemic species. The annual wildflower explosion in late spring is as spectacular as anywhere in southern Europe, especially in areas where the rural exodus has ensured that much of the land has never seen the use of pesticides.

For a list of 300 of the more common species to be found in Andalucía, with common and Latin names, visit www.cicerone.co.uk/803/resources.

Wildlife

Vertebrates are less easy to spot but are also present. Along with the grazing goats, sheep, cattle and Iberian pigs you may see squirrels, hares, rabbits, deer, wild boar, otters and mongoose. Ibex (*Capra pyrenaica hispanica*) are making a rapid comeback in Andalucía and these can often be spotted on the more abrupt slopes of the Sierra del Pinar, the Lagarín peak close to El Gastor and to both sides of the Líbar valley south of Montejaque.

Andalucía has a long roll call when it comes to reptiles. Of its many

Red squirrel, Sciurus vulgaris

species of snakes just one is poisonous; the Lataste viper (easily identified by the distinctive zigzag stripe that runs the length of its back with a line of black dots to each side). However, they are very timid reptiles and the chance of spotting them is extremely remote. Iberian and wall lizards are common, as are chameleons.

GEOLOGY

The Baetic range of mountains take their name from Baetica, the name given by the Romans to southeastern Spain. The mountains owe their origin to the orogenic belt – also known as the Gibraltar arc – that was formed as the African plate pushed beneath Iberia during the Miocene era. Land that once lay beneath the ocean was pushed upwards while buckling and the collapse of mountain belts during the Palaeozoic and Mesozoic era brought deeply buried rocks to the surface. Thus sandstone, conglomerate and limestone along with metamorphic rock and peridotites, are a common feature of the Serranía de Ronda.

The region is home to some of the finest karst limestone scenery in Europe while the action of rainfall on this highly soluble rock has created some of Spain's largest cave systems and potholes. Lying along the border of two huge tectonic plates, Andalucía has been subject to many earthquakes. Many of Ronda's buildings, including its principal church,

suffered severe damage in the earthquake of 1570 while the Lisbon earthquake of 1755 also damaged the town and several of the region's many churches.

ANDALUCÍAN HISTORICAL OVERVIEW

The history of the sierras of southern Spain is inextricably linked to their position at the extreme south of Europe, looking east to Europe, west to the Atlantic and with just a short stretch of water separating their southernmost tip from Africa. This is a land at the crossroads between two continents, and at the same time part of one of the richest spheres of trade the world has ever known: the Mediterranean Basin.

Ancient times

Many vestiges in the Ronda mountains – burial sites, cave paintings, flint-knapping sites and countless axes, arrow heads and pottery shards – bear witness to the area having seen constant human passage, and settlement, during the prehistoric era. There's substantial evidence to suggest that it was along the valleys leading north towards Ronda that man first passed from Africa into Europe, and nowhere is there a more remarkable testimony to the region's prehistory than at La Cueva de la Pileta close to Benaoján (see Walk 13). A series of remarkable paintings within its underground cavern system has been dated to the

El Dolmen del Charcón (Walk 27)

Palaeolithic, Mesolithic and Neolithic periods while several dolmens in the area (see Walk 27) bear witness to an emerging funerary cult.

The early inhabitants of the Iberian peninsula were later dominated by waves of population from the north, giving rise to the Celtiberian culture. These early pastoralists established fortified settlements throughout the peninsular and it was they, some 600 years before Christ, who first settled the high plateau at Arunda, from which Ronda takes its name.

During the pre-Christian era Phoenicians established trading posts in Málaga and Cádiz, including one just to the west of Ronda, attracted by rich mineral deposits and fertile agricultural lands that lay inland from the Mediterranean. But it was under the Romans, who ruled Spain from the 3rd century BC to the 5th century AD that the region began to take on its present day character. They established copper and silver mines, planted olives and vines, cleared land for agriculture and built towns, roads, aqueducts, bridges, theatres and baths while imposing their native language and customs. Although Ronda had a sizeable Roman settlement, with waters channelled down to the town from the Sierra de las Nieves, a much larger urbis was built at Acinipo, on a high plateau to the west of the present day town. The settlement was large enough to have a theatre, baths and a forum, and even came to mint its own coins.

Meanwhile, just south of Grazalema, close to Ubrique, Ocurris also grew in importance as testified by the existence of a sizeable mausoleum, baths and massive defensive walls. The lands around Ocurris were

19

linked with those to the north by road, a large section of which remains intact today (you will see parts of it on Walk 20). This in turn connected to others that linked the cities of Roman Andalucía: the coastal settlements of Baelo Claudio and Malaca (present day Málaga) along with Itálica (Sevilla) and Corduba (Córdoba). Walk 22 from Grazalema to Benaocáz can be extended to include a 2km section of the Roman road and you see shorter sections of this ancient byway on the Grazalema northern circuit (Walk 20).

By the 5th century the Roman Empire was in free fall, at a time when the centre of its power had shifted eastwards to what would become Byzantium. Weakened by internal division, it was unable to defend itself from attacks from the tribes it had once ruled in northern and central Europe. In 402 the Visigoths under Alaric sacked Rome, whilst the Iberian peninsula saw the passage of Vandals and Alans before the Visigoths established a kingdom, with its capital in Toledo, that would last until the early 8th century.

Moorish Andalucía and the Christian Reconquest

If Rome laid the foundations of Andalucían society in its broadest sense, these were shallow in comparison to those bequeathed in the wake of the expeditionary force that sailed

Ronda and its Moorish battlements, seen from the north (Walk 1)

from the North African coast across the Strait in 711 under the Moorish commander Tariq. Landing close to Gibraltar, Tariq's army of Moslems decisively defeated the ruling Visigoths in their first encounter. What had been little more than a loose confederation of tribes, deprived of their ruler, offered little resistance to the advance of Islam across Spain. By 713 Ronda was occupied by the Moors and later became the capital of the district of Takaruna.

It was only when Charles Martel defeated the Moorish army close to the banks of the Loire in 732 that the tide began to turn and the Moors looked to consolidate their conquests rather than venture deeper into Europe. Moorish Spain's golden age took hold in the 8th century by which time the centre of their power had shifted from Toledo further south to Córdoba. It was here that Jews, Christians and Moors established a modus vivendi the likes of which has rarely been replicated, and which yielded one of the richest artistic periods Europe has known. Philosophers, musicians, poets, mathematicians and astronomers from all three religions helped establish Córdoba as a centre for learning second to no other in the West, at the centre of a trading network that stretched from Africa to the Middle East and through Spain to northern Europe. And it was during the great Cordoban Caliphate that Berber tribesmen and farmers – who found the mountains in the Ronda

area similar to those they had left behind in North Africa – established settlements in a region that provided such rich grazing for their flocks.

However, the Moorish Kingdom was always under threat, and the Reconquest – a process that was to last more than 800 years – gradually gained momentum as the Christian kingdoms of central and northern Spain became more unified. Córdoba fell in 1031 following which the great Caliphate splintered into a number of smaller Taifa kingdoms. During this period the small fiefdom of Ronda was able to punch well above its weight, a near-impenetrable eagle's nest set atop steep cliffs with a massive lower line of fortifications. Ruled over by the feared Banu Ifren tribe of Berber hillsmen, they frequently and openly opposed Caliphal orders, secure in a mountain refuge that could only have been taken by mounting a campaign with a huge army.

The Moors clung on for another 250 years, now ruled by the Nasrid dynasty of sultans in Granada, but by the late 15th century the settlements along the Sultanate's western frontier (La Frontera) were under threat. Zahara de la Sierra fell to the Christian armies in the early 1481, then Grazalema and Ronda in 1485. With an unprotected western border the Nasrids knew that they were living on borrowed time. The Christians took Málaga and Vélez in 1487 and finally Granada in 1492.

Post-Reconquista

If ever anybody was in the right place at the right time it was the Genoese adventurer Cristobal Colon, aka Christopher Columbus, who was in the Christian camp when Granada capitulated. His petition to the Catholic monarchs for funding for an expedition to sail west in order to reach the East fell on fertile soil. The discovery of America, and along with it the fabulous riches that made their way back to a Spain newly united under Habsburg rule, was to usher in Spain's *Siglo de Oro* or Golden Age.

Spain's empire soon stretched from the Caribbean through Central and South America and on to the Philippines; riches flowed back from the colonies at a time when Sevilla and Cádiz numbered among the wealthiest cities in Europe. The most obvious manifestation of this wealth – and nowhere more so than in Andalucía – were the palaces, churches, monasteries and convents that were built during this period: never again would the country see such generous patronage of the Arts.

Ronda saw considerable growth in the years following the Reconquista, repopulated by Christians from central and northern Spain. A number of churches and convents were built while parts of the Moorish Mosque were incorporated into the cathedral of Santa María. By the end of the 16th century the town's growing importance was recognised when Ronda saw the creation of its Real Maestranza, one of just four such bodies that were established to school Christian knights in the art of horsemanship. The newly learned skills proved to be a vital factor when the Moriscos, small groups of Moors who had stayed on after the Reconquest, rose up against their Christian oppressors at the end of the 16th century.

If the final campaign against the Moors ended in victory, Spain's position at the centre of the world stage would soon be under threat. A series of wars in Europe depleted Spain's credibility as well as the state coffers and by the late 17th century Spanish power was in free fall. By the end of the War of the Spanish Succession the country had become a second-rate power with greatly reduced influence in European affairs, a situation which was exacerbated by three major outbreaks of bubonic plague which took a great toll on Ronda and the surrounding villages.

By the 18th century the Spanish population, and that of Ronda, was expanding once again. Ronda gradually expanded north, east and west of the original Moorish hilltop settlement. Urban growth was facilitated when the Puente Nuevo was completed in 1793, giving easy access to the plateau just west of its plunging gorge. The town's bullring was completed in the same year, and it was here that the art of fighting bulls on foot was established and refined by the great Romero dynasty of fighters.

A period of relative prosperity in Spain and in the sierras of the south came to an end when the Bonapartist forces invaded Spain from Portugal in 1808. The Peninsular War, known to Spaniards as La Guerra de la Independencia, had a devastating effect on the country. This was particularly marked in Andalucía where the French forces were gradually pushed eastwards across Spain. Several villages in the Sierra, most notably Montejaque and Algodonales, put up fierce resistance to the French forces, an opposition that is still celebrated with annual re-enactments of the battles that were fought. During the war several of the region's oldest churches, chapels, and civic buildings saw great damage at the hands of Bonaparte's retreating army.

Ronda seen from below (Walk 6)

The 20th and 21st centuries

Spain remained a spent force into the 19th century and further violent conflict in the early 20th saw the increasing polarisation of Spain's population into right-wing and left-wing groupings. By 1936 – following the election of a radical Popular Front Coalition government and the declaration of the Second Republic – the die was cast and Franco embarked on his 'crusade' to re-establish the traditional order in Spain. The ensuing conflict – the Spanish Civil War – lasted for three years, during which an estimated 500,000 Spaniards lost their lives.

Andalucía and the villages in the mountains close to Ronda, where the political creeds of socialism, communism and anarchy had a huge following, fell early in the war to Franco's armies. As was the case throughout Spain, Ronda and the surrounding villages saw bloody reprisals and assassinations on both sides of a deeply polarised political spectrum. The eventual victory of the Nationalists in 1939 led to Franco's consolidation and centralisation of power and the establishment of an authoritarian state that remained until his death in 1975. Spain's peripheral regions, along with their language and culture, once again became subject to centralised government under which any attempt to nurture differences in culture and language was severely repressed. Andalucía, which had been a centre of radical, left-wing dissent in the years leading up to the Civil War, was systematically marginalised by Franco's reactionary and autarchic regime.

Franco had hoped that King Juan Carlos, who he'd appointed as his predecessor prior to his death, would continue to govern much in his image; but the young king knew which way the tide was running and facilitated the creation of a new constitution for Spain and, along with it, parliamentary democracy. Andalucía, as was the case for several other regions of Spain, saw the creation of an autonomous *junta*, or government, based in Sevilla.

The 80s, 90s and noughties were very good years for Andalucía following Spain's entry into the EEC, during which time it saw its infrastructure rapidly transformed. New roads, schools, hospitals and hotels were built, along with a high-speed train line from Sevilla to Madrid. The huge construction boom put money into many a working person's pocket; Andalucía had never had it so good.

Tourism continues to be a major motor of the Andalucían economy, along with the construction industry, fuelled by ex-pats setting up home in the south and other foreigners buying holiday homes and flats. The Costa del Sol, especially, has always been a huge source of employment for Ronda and the surrounding villages. But the economic downturn has hit the region hard and Andalucía currently has an unemployment rate among its adult workforce of almost 35% – the highest in Spain – while among young people that percentage is almost double.

However, at the time of writing (2017) there are signs that the building industry – a major part of the region's beleaguered economy and a yardstick for the rest of the economy – is beginning to recover as the familiar clunk of the cement mixer makes a welcome return to the backstreets of the sierras of Ronda and Grazalema.

WHEN TO GO

As a general rule, the best time to walk in the Ronda mountains is from March through to June and from September to late October. This is when you're likely to encounter mild, sunny weather: warm enough to dine al fresco yet not so hot as to make temperature an additional challenge. Wildflowers are at their best in late April/early May and this is the time when many walking companies plan their walks.

Most walkers avoid July and August when temperatures regularly reach the mid to high 30s, making walking much more of a challenge. That said, if you limit yourself to shorter circuits, get going early and take plenty of water you can still enjoy walking in high summer.

If you're prepared to risk seeing some rain then winter is a wonderful time to be out walking in Andalucía, especially from December to February when rainfall is generally less than in November, March and April.

Wildflower meadow close to Ronda in the month of May (Walk 17)

GETTING THERE AND GETTING AROUND

By air

Sevilla and Jerez are both less than a two-hour drive from Ronda and Grazalema and have regular flights from the UK. Málaga has charter flights from all major cities in the UK as well as scheduled flights with British Airlines and Iberia. There are also good connections between several UK cities and Gibraltar from where you're a little over two hours' drive from Ronda.

By car

Car hire in Spain is inexpensive when compared to that in other European destinations, and the major companies are represented at all airports. Prices for car hire ex-Málaga tend to be lower. Public transport is surprisingly limited in the Sierra so hiring a car will make trip planning far easier, especially when trailheads are away from the village centres like most of those described in the Sierra de las Nieves. It's possible to rent a car in Ronda (see listings in Appendix B). Spanish speakers could also take advantage of car shares via www. blablacar.com which is hugely popular in southern Spain.

By train and bus

There are regular buses from Málaga, Sevilla and Jerez to Ronda.

Three trains leave Málaga on weekdays for Ronda, two of which involve a change in Bobadilla. There are very few buses between Ronda and the Sierra de Grazalema and the Sierra de las Nieves.

ACCOMMODATION

If Andalucían tourism was once all about beach and hotel tourism the past 30 years have seen a huge growth in the numbers of visitors who come to discover its walking trails. Prices in the mountains are generally low in comparison to the hotels of the coastal resorts. As a rule of thumb, for €50–€75 you'll be able to find a decent hotel room for two with its own bath or shower room, and breakfast will often be included.

The contact details of recommended hotels, hostels and B&Bs in and around the villages where walks begin or end are listed, by region, in

Cartajima in the evening light (Walk 10)

Appendix C. All listings have been visited by the author and all are clean and welcoming. Most offer breakfast as well as evening meals while many places can prepare picnics, given prior warning.

Nearly every hotel in Andalucía is listed on www.booking.com, where, in theory, you'll always get the lowest price. Bear in mind though, that by contacting the hotel directly you'll be saving them the commission they'd pay to the website, so they're sometimes happy to cut out the third party and offer a lower price. Hotels may also have special offers posted on their own websites. However, both booking.com and TripAdvisor (www.tripadvisor.co.uk) can be a good starting point if you wish to read about other guests' experiences at any given place.

Hotels in Andalucía make extensive use of marble. It's a perfect material for the searing heat of the summer, but in winter marble floors can be icy cold. Pack a pair of slippers: they can be a godsend if travelling when the weather is cold. And when sleeping in budget options during cold weather it's worth ringing ahead to ask the owners if they'd mind switching on the heating before your arrival. Remember too, that cheaper hostels often don't provide soap or shampoo.

When checking in at hotel receptions expect to be asked for your passport. Once details have been noted down, Spanish law requires that it's returned to you.

EATING OUT IN SOUTHERN SPAIN

Although it may not be known as a gourmet destination, you can eat very well in Andalucía if you're prepared to leave a few of your preconceptions at home. Ronda, as you might expect of a major tourist destination, has a huge range of restaurants for all budgets. Much of the food on the menu in mountain village restaurants is stored in a deep freezer and microwaved when ordered – the exceptions to the rule being the freshly prepared *tapas* that you'll see displayed in a glass cabinet in nearly every bar and restaurant. These can provide a delicious meal in themselves.

A tapa (taking its name from the lid or 'tapa' that once covered the jars in which they were stored) has come to mean a saucer-sized plate of any one dish, served to accompany an aperitif before lunch or dinner. If you wish to have more of any particular tapa you can order a *ración* (a large plateful) or a *media ración* (half that amount). Two or three raciónes shared between two, along with a mixed salad, make a substantial and inexpensive meal.

When eating à la carte don't expect there to be much in the way of vegetables served with any meal: they just don't tend to figure in Andalucían cuisine. However, no meal in southern Spain is complete without some form of salad, which is where Andalucíans get their vitamin intake. And fresh fruit is always available as a dessert.

Bear in mind that there's always a *menú del día* (set menu) available at lunchtime – even if waiters will try to push you towards eating à la carte – and as a result of the recent economic downturn many restaurants now also offer the menú del día in the evenings. Although you have less choice – generally two or three starters, mains and desserts – the fact that set menus are often prepared on the day, using fresh rather than frozen ingredients, means this can often be the best way to eat.

Expect to pay around €10 for a three-course set menu in a village restaurant which normally includes a soft drink, beer or a glass of wine. When eating à la carte you can expect to pay around €20–€25 per head for a three-course meal including beverages, while a tapas-style meal will be slightly less. Tipping after a meal is common although no offence will be taken should you not leave a gratuity when paying smaller sums for drinks at bars.

The southern Spanish eat later than is the custom in northern Europe. Lunch is not generally available until 2.00pm and restaurants rarely open before 7.00pm. A common lament among walkers is that breakfast is often not served at hotels until 9.00am, although village bars are open from 8am. If you're keen to make an early start, pack a Thermos. Most hotels will be happy to fill it the night before, and you can always buy the makings of your own breakfast from a village shop.

Breakfasts in hotels can be disappointing and are often better taken at a local bar. Most serve far better coffee than you'll get at a hotel, freshly squeezed rather than boxed orange juice, and *una tostada con aceite y tomate* – toast served with tomato and olive oil – can be a great way to start your walking day.

When shopping for the makings of your picnic, be aware that village shops are generally open from 9.00am to 2.00pm and then 5.30pm to 8.30pm. Many smaller shops will be happy to make you up a *bocadillo* or sandwich using the ingredients of your choice.

LANGUAGE

Visitors to inland Andalucía often express surprise at how little English is spoken, where even in restaurants and hotels a working knowledge of English is the exception rather than the norm. In addition, the Spanish spoken in southern Spain – Andaluz – can be difficult to understand even if you have a command of basic Spanish: it's spoken at lightning speed, with the end of words often left unpronounced.

It's worth picking up a phrasebook before you travel. And be prepared to gesticulate: you always get there in the end.

MONEY

Most travellers to Spain still consider that the cost of their holiday essentials – food, travel and accommodation – is considerably lower than in northern Europe. You can still find a decent meal for two, with drinks, for around €40; and €60 can buy you a comfortable hotel room for two.

Every start point village in this guide has an ATM, and you'll generally be able to pay in shops, restaurants and hotels with a credit card (although you may be asked for some form of identity that matches the name on your card). Be aware that you'll often be asked for credit card details when booking a hotel room by phone.

PHONES AND WI-FI

While most of Spain now has good mobile coverage for all major phone operators, there are still quite a few gaps in the mountains where many of these walks will be taking you. Even

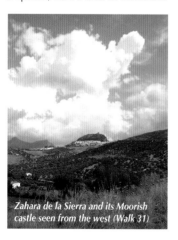

Zahara de la Sierra and its Moorish castle seen from the west (Walk 31)

The final ascent to the summit of Coros (Walk 24)

so, it's always wise to have a charged phone in your daypack, preloaded with emergency contact numbers (see Appendix B, Useful contacts).

Wi-fi coverage is available in most hotels and is nearly always free of charge.

WHAT TO TAKE

The two most important things to take with you when you walk in Andalucía are:

- water – carry a minimum of two litres. During the warmer months the greatest potential dangers are heat exhaustion and dehydration. Wear loose-fitting clothes, a hat, and keep drinking.
- comfortable, broken-in walking boots – no walk is enjoyable when you've got blisters.

With safety in mind, you should also carry the following:

- hat and sun block
- map and compass
- Swiss Army Knife or similar
- torch and whistle
- fully charged mobile phone (even though coverage can be patchy in the mountains)
- waterproofs, according to season
- fleece or jumper (temperatures can drop rapidly at the top of the higher passes)
- first aid kit including antihistamine cream, plasters, bandage, plastic skin for blisters
- water purifying tablets
- chocolate/sweets or glucose tablets
- handheld GPS device (if you have one)

29

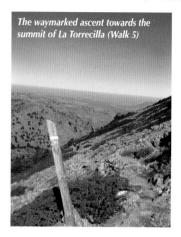

The waymarked ascent towards the summit of La Torrecilla (Walk 5)

MAPS

Under each general section I've recommended the best map available for the area, and Appendix B includes the full contact details of companies from which you can buy these maps. All of the Spanish retailers will send maps *contra reembolso* (payment on receipt) to addresses within Spain.

In Andalucía the best places to order maps are LTC in Sevilla (www.ltcideas.es/index.php/mapas and Mapas y Compañia in Málaga (www.mapasycia.es); in Madrid the best places are La Tienda Verde (www.tiendaverde.es), Centro Nacional de Información Geográfica (www.cnig.es) and Desnivel (www.libreriadesnivel.com). In the UK the best places for maps, which can be ordered online, are Stanfords (www.stanfords.co.uk) and the Map Shop (www.themapshop.co.uk).

STAYING SAFE

When heading off on any walk, always let at least one person know where you're going and the time at which you expect to return.

Log the following emergency telephone numbers into your mobile:

- 112 Emergency services general number
- 062 Guardía Civil (police)
- 061 Medical emergencies
- 080 Fire brigade

In addition to the usual precautions to take, there are a few things to remember when walking in Andalucía:

- **Water** – be aware that in dry years some of the springs that are mentioned in this guide can slow to little more than a trickle or dry up altogether. Always carry plenty of water, and consider keeping a supply of water purification tablets in your daypack.
- **Fire** – in the dry months the hillsides of Andalucía become a vast tinderbox. Be very careful if you smoke or use a camping stove.
- **Hunting areas** – signs for '*coto*' or '*coto privado de caza*' designate an area where hunting is permitted in season and not that you're entering private property. There could also be bulls of the fighting variety. Cotos are normally marked by a small rectangular sign divided into a white-and-black triangle.
- **Close all gates** – so livestock don't stray. You'll come across

La Sierra Cabrilla seen on the descent towards El Burgo (Walk 4)

some extraordinary gate-closing devices! They can take time, patience and effort to open and close.

USING THIS GUIDE

The 32 walks in this guide are divided into three sections. For each region the walks will introduce you to the most attractive areas of the particular region and lead you to its most interesting villages.

Each section begins with an overview of the area, including information about its geography, plants and wildlife, climate and culture. This is followed by details of tourist information and maps relevant to the walks described in the section.

The information boxes at the start of each walk provide the essential statistics: start point (and finish point if the walk is linear), total distance covered, ascent and descent, grade or rating, and estimated walking time. They also include, where relevant, notes on transport and access, and en route refreshments options (not including springs). The subsequent walk introduction gives you a feel for what any given itinerary involves.

The route description, together with the individual route map, should allow you to follow these walks without difficulty. Places and features on the map are highlighted in bold in the route description to aid navigation. However, you should always carry a compass and, ideally, the

Cortes de la Frontera seen through the trees on the descent towards the village (Walk 15)

recommended map of the area; a handheld GPS device is always an excellent second point of reference (see 'GPS tracks', below).

Water springs have been included in the route descriptions but bear in mind that following dry periods they may be all but non-existent. When the term 'stream bed' is mentioned in walk descriptions do bear in mind that for a large part of the year most of these are dry while after heavy rainfall they could be in spate. You will always need to be the judge as to whether these are safe to cross.

The walks

The walks in this book are generally of three types. Most of those described are circular itineraries, beginning and ending in beautiful mountain villages where there's some kind of accommodation available.

A few are linear walks linking two villages where public transport is available, at a convenient time, back to your point of departure.

There are four there-and-back routes where these walks are sufficiently special that such doubling up doesn't detract from the beauty and interest of the walk.

Grading

Walks are graded as follows:
- Easy – shorter walks with little height gain
- Easy/Medium – mid-length walks with little steep climbing

- Medium – mid-length walks with some steep up and downhill sections
- Medium/Difficult – longer routes with a number of steep up and downhill sections.

If you're reasonably fit you should experience no difficulty with any of these routes. For walks classed as Medium/Difficult, the most important thing is to allow plenty of time and take a good supply of water. And remember that what can be an easy walk in cooler weather becomes a much more difficult challenge in the heat. This rating system assumes the sort of weather you're likely to encounter in winter, spring or autumn in Andalucía.

Times

These timings are based on an average walking pace, without breaks. You'll soon see if it equates roughly to your own pace, and can then adjust timings accordingly. On all routes you should allow at least an additional hour-and-a-half if you intend to break for food, photography and rest stops.

Definition of terms

The terms used in this guide are intended to be as unambiguous as possible. In walk descriptions, 'track' denotes any thoroughfare wide enough to permit vehicle access, and 'path' is used to describe any that is wide enough only for pedestrians and animals.

Path lined with grey cistus close to Ronda (Walk 7)

You'll see references in many walks to 'GR' and 'PR'. GR stands for Gran Recorrido or long-distance footpath; these routes are marked with red and white waymarking. PR stands for Pequeño Recorrido or short-distance footpath and these routes are marked with yellow and white waymarking.

GPS tracks

The GPX trail files for all of the walks featured in this guide are available as free downloads from Cicerone (www.cicerone.co.uk/892/GPX) and via the author's website (www.guyhunter watts.com).

By using a programme such as Garmin's BaseCamp you can download the files to your desktop, import them into the programme and then transfer them to your handheld device. You can download Basecamp

Waymarking beneath the Ronda cliff face (Walk 6)

for Mac and PC at www.garmin.com/garmin/cms/us/onthetrail/basecamp.

GPX files are provided in good faith, but neither the author nor Cicerone can accept responsibility for their accuracy. Your first point of reference should always be the walking notes themselves.

RONDA AND THE SIERRA DE LAS NIEVES

Looking south across the bowl of the Ronda valley (Walk 6)

The footpath leading up to Los Enamorados, Sierra de las Nieves (Walk 2)

Rising steeply upwards to the east of Ronda the rugged massif of the Sierra de las Nieves is the wildest and least visited of the three walking regions in this guide. While most walks described in this area require a longer drive to arrive at their start point, the additional effort will be amply rewarded on walks where you'll encounter few other hikers and where there's a good chance that you'll have the trail all to yourself.

After gaining limited protection when designated a hunting reserve in the 1950s, some 300 square kilometres of the park were given Parque Natural status in 1989 while in 1995 an area more than three times that size was declared a Biosphere Reserve by UNESCO. And as this guide goes to press the area is due to be become a 'National' rather than a 'Natural' park with the additional protection and funding that the designation implies.

As the name Sierra de las Nieves suggests, the mountains are often snow clad during the winter months when weather systems from the north and west run up against this formidable mountain barrier. La Torrecilla at 1919m is the highest peak in western Andalucía and if you climb it at any time between November and March you may well encounter snow (an ascent of the peak is described in Walk 5).

Due to the relative isolation and abrupt topography of the region this is one of the areas of southern Spain where you're least aware of the hand of man in fashioning the landscape. This was never an area that lent itself easily to cultivation: the few isolated farmsteads you come across on the walks described in this book speak of an era when it was barely possible to eke out an existence on the land. By the early 1960s most of these remote cortijos were abandoned, at a time when emigration was bleeding Andalucía of its smallholders and *jornaleros* (day labourers).

Given the park's newly protected status, all economic activity is now strictly controlled within its confines, and the region's forest mass – which was depleted by centuries of industry and forest fire – is slowly recovering. On most routes described in this guide you'll see evidence of reafforestation projects.

GEOLOGY

The Sierra's geological make-up is diverse with limestone predominant and marlstone also present. All the more common features of limestone scenery are present in the park including karrens (areas of exposed limestone to which dissolution imparts a pavement-like appearance), caves and potholes, as well as some of the finest karst (deeply weathered landscape formed by the action of rainfall and the subsequent acidic dissolution of soluble rock like limestone, dolomite and gypsum) scenery in Andalucía, while many of the rock's most remarkable features lie deep underground, carved out over the millennia by the action of rainwater. There are numerous cave systems and potholes including the deepest in Andalucía, the Sima

GESM: to date it has been explored to a depth of over 1000 metres. A smaller percentage of igneous rock is also present in the form of peridotites and serpentinites as are metamorphic schists and marbles.

PLANTS AND WILDLIFE

The botanical jewel of the park is unquestionably the pinsapo or Spanish fir (*Abies pinsapo*). The world's largest stand of this Ice Age relic fills a valley just to the west of Alozaina (Walk 1 cuts through this hauntingly beautiful forest.) Severely depleted stands of gall and holm oaks are also being nursed back to healthier life, helped by restrictions that have been introduced on the grazing of goats. The park is also home to some of the most extensive stands of arbutus and yew in southern Spain while wildflowers are spectacular in their abundance: these are at their best between April and May, thriving in a landscape that has seen scant use of pesticides. If you'd like a list of the more common species visit www. cicerone.co.uk/803/resources

Although more spectacular as an avian event further west, part of the annual bird migration between Europe and northwestern Africa passes over the park where there are rich rewards for ornithologists. The chances of spotting raptors are high all year round, although not quite as easy as in the Grazalema mountains further west. Griffon vultures (*Gyps fulvus*) are occasionally seen while the chances of seeing booted and short-toed eagles are much higher, and with very good luck, golden eagles and Egyptian vultures. Lammergeiers, which were once a common sighting in the park, are no longer present. If you'd like a list of the more common species visit www.cicerone.co.uk/803/resources

If hunting took its toll on the mammal population this, like the forest cover, is also making a comeback. Most notable is the ibex (*Capra pyrenaica hispanica*), which you'll have a good chance of observing on most walks described in the region. Further to the south otters can be seen in the upper reaches of the Río Verde while you may come across grazing roe deer. Genets and Egyptian mongoose are also present along with an extensive roll call of lizards and snakes.

VILLAGES

The villages that give access to several of the best walks in the Sierra lie mostly along it northeastern limits. The small whitewashed village of El Burgo is the author's favourite and is a great base for walks on the eastern side of the park (see Appendix C). The workaday village of Alozaina, close to the start points of Walks 1 and 2, sees far fewer visitors though it does have a simple hostel and a handful of restaurants. A little further to the south, but also within easy access of the walks in the east of the park, the ancient spa town of Tolox is worth a visit and has an excellent small hotel

Ronda's most famous landmark, the Puente Nuevo (Walk 8)

built on a bluff high above the village, with wonderful food, kindly management and huge bedrooms (see Appendix C).

RONDA

If these villages have rather less of historical interest, Ronda numbers among Spain and Europe's most fascinating towns: it's for good reason that it has become one of the most popular tourist destinations in Spain both for walkers and non-walkers. Dubbed Ciudad Soñada by its local council, Ronda can truly lay claim to being a Town of Dreams with a breathtaking physical setting.

The town fans out along a high plateau through which, over the millennia, the Guadalevín river has cut a deep gorge. Known simply as El Tajo by locals, this plunging abyss is spanned by an extraordinary bridge, the Puente Nuevo, an architectural arabesque that can't fail to excite even the most travel-weary eyes. A favoured destination on the Grand Tour during the 19th century, the town attracted poets, actors, painters and aesthetes: the likes of Rilke, David Roberts, Orson Welles, Hemingway and Bomberg were all bewitched by its beauty while James Joyce waxed lyrically about the gorge on the final page of *Ulysses*.

The town has a huge range of accommodation for all budgets (see Appendix C) and if you were to make the town your base for a walking holiday you'd be within easy driving range of at least 20 of the walks described in this book.

It's worth dropping by at the Tourist Office in Ronda (opposite the eastern side of the bullring) to pick up a free pamphlet which lists the opening times of all of the town's historic monuments and museums. If you'd like an up-to-date list of the author's favourite restaurants and tapas bars in the town, along with recommendations of where best to eat in the nearby villages, email the author via the contact form on www.guyhunterwatts.com

MAPS

The Tourist Office has an excellent free map of Ronda which is perfect for the historical tour of Ronda described in Walk 8. For other walks described in this section the best map is the Penibetica 1:40000 Parque Natural Sierra de las Nieves. The next best map which also covers all walks apart from a tiny section of Walk 7 is the 1:50000 I.N.G. quadrant Ronda 1051.

TAXIS

- Ronda: main taxi rank 952 872 316; other recommended drivers – Luis 649 362 437, Esteban 606 986 666
- El Burgo: Paco 952 160 210

WALK 1

*Puerto de Caucón circuit via
El Tajo de la Caina*

Start/Finish	Mirador Puerto de Caucón (also called Mirador de Luis Ceballos), near Yunquera
Distance	7km
Ascent/Descent	475m
Grade	Medium
Time	2hr 20min
Refreshments	None en route
Access	From Ronda take the A-366 via El Burgo to Yunquera. Arriving at a roundabout at the entrance to the village turn right then follow signs for 6.7km to the Mirador Puerto de Caucón (or Mirador de Luis Ceballos)

This exhilarating half-day walk leads through one of La Sierra de la Nieves' largest stands of Spanish firs (*Abies pinsapo*) to the towering cliff face, then the summit, of El Tajo de la Caina. This vertical face numbers among the park's most impressive feats of Nature, rising sheer above the spring of the same name for almost 200m. A bluff just beyond the spring provides a stunning promontory to rest before climbing to La Caina's summit (1394m) before you return to the walk's start point by way of the upper reaches of the Pinsapar de los Zarzalones.

The walk can be shortened by returning via a shorter, marked trail that loops back to Puerto de Caucón from La Era de los Gamones. Set time aside to gulp in the views from La Caina as well from the Mirador Puerto de Caucón from where a vast panorama opens out to the south and east which, on clear days, encompasses the distant peaks of the Sierra Nevada.

The walk begins at the parking area at the Mirador Puerto de Caucón. Exit the parking area at its western end past a commemorative plaque to Luis Ceballos following a sign for 'Senderos 30m'.

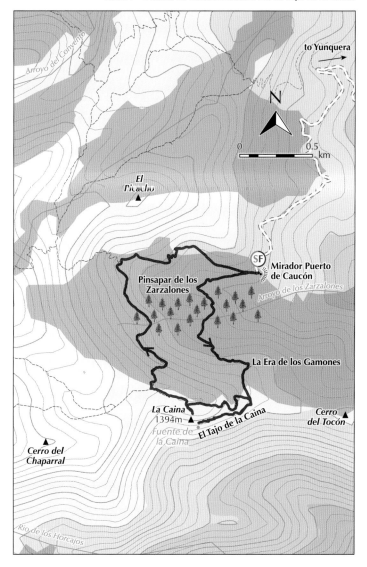

The view east from the Mirador Puerto de Caucón

Luis Ceballos (1896–1967) was a botanist who in the 1920s and 1930s documented the flora of the Ronda and Grazalema mountains. He was active in protecting the remaining stands of pinsapos in the Sierra as well as initiating projects for their reafforestation.

Reaching a fork after 30m angle left at a sign, 'Sendero Caucón-Tajo de la Caina'. The path loops steeply down through juniper to enter a stand of pinsapos where reafforestation is taking place. After crossing the stream bed of the **Arroyo de los Zarzalones** the path climbs, passing a signboard about the trees of the Pinsapar de los Zarzalones before crossing a low rise. After descending it climbs once again in a series of tight loops. As the trees thin out the Mirador Puerto de Caucón comes into sight down beneath you.

Reaching a ridge top and an old threshing platform, **La Era de los Gamones**, cut right following a sign for 'Tajo de la Caina/Vistas Panorámicas 750m'. The path climbs

El Tajo de la Caina's southern face

through enormous pinsapos before reaching an open tract of ground where, heading straight ahead, you reach the *mirador* (viewing point) and a sign, 'Fin de Sendero' (55min).

From here cut right past a sign warning of steep drops to one side of the path. Follow a narrow path beneath the southern face of a cliff over a series of knolls, all with soaring views to the south. Sticking close to the cliff face you reach the **Fuente de la Caina**, which emerges from a cleft in the cliff face. ▶

Some 50m beyond the spring is a perfect place for a break.

From here retrace your footsteps back to the sign, 'Fin de Sendero', then head back towards the Era de los Gamones for 75m to a sign marking 'Vistas Panorámicas'. Here bear left up through the pinsapos. The path, initially indistinct, adopts a westerly course before angling back

43

round to the east and passing through a breach in the rocks. Cairns mark your way. The path winds back to the west before reaching flatter ground.

Optional ascent of La Caina

Here, cutting hard to the left, you could make your way up to the highest point of **La Caina** (1394m) (1hr 20min). Be aware that there are sheer, unprotected drops just a few metres to the south. Once you have visited the summit, retrace your steps back to the main path.

Maintaining your course west across La Caina, parallel to the top of the cliff face, you pass just to the right of another old *era* (threshing floor). Continuing on the same course you pass a sign which reads 'Era 120m'. Some 5m beyond the sign you reach a three-way junction. Ignoring waymarking to the left, branch right past a wooden post with a large cairn at its base. A clear footpath leads back down in a series of loops into the **Pinsapar de los Zarzalones**.

After a steep descent the path bears left, levels then adopts a northwesterly course as the Mirador Puerto de Caucón comes into view once again, still running on through the pinsapos. After passing in front of a steep outcrop of limestone the path loops round to the right as it contours round the upper reaches of the valley of the **Arroyo de los Zarzalones**. After crossing three of the stream's tributaries it runs east along the northern side of the valley where reafforestation is taking place. Some 30m after passing the fork where you earlier forked left you return to the parking area of the **Mirador Puerto de Caucón** (2hr 20min).

WALK 2
El Peñon de los Enamorados circuit

Start/Finish	Mirador del Puerto del Saucillo, 6km from Yunquera
Distance	12.5km
Ascent/Descent	800m
Grade	Medium/Difficult
Time	4hr
Refreshments	None en route
Access	From Ronda take the A-366 via El Burgo to Yunquera. Arriving at a roundabout just beyond km33 at the entrance to the village turn right at a sign for Miradores then follow the track for 6km to Puerto del Saucillo.
Warning	The path along the lower section of the Cañada de los Hornillos is overgrown in parts so it's best to have long trousers or gaiters in your pack.

This walk has to be a contender in the 'best hikes in Andalucía' stakes. It takes you, by way of narrow mountain footpaths, through the heart of a mesmerisingly beautiful stand of Spanish firs (*Abies pinsapo*), offers vast views to all points of the compass and can be combined with an easy scramble to the rocky summit of Los Enamorados (1775m), one of the Sierra de las Nieves' most emblematic peaks. The track that leads in to the start point of the walk is an adventure in its own right, leading you in a series of sharp hairpins up to the viewing platform of Puerto del Saucillo. Bear in mind that the wind-chill factor can cause temperatures to drop rapidly in the colder months along the exposed ridge that runs to either side of the Puerto del Cuco.

The walk begins at a signboard marked 'Sendero Puerto Saucillo-Torrecilla' at the southern side of the parking area, to one side of the Mirador del Puerto del Saucillo. Facing west, take the path marked 'PRA351'. Climbing through a stand of pinsapos and Mediterranean pines you shortly pass a signboard, 'Pozo de Nieve': it's worth

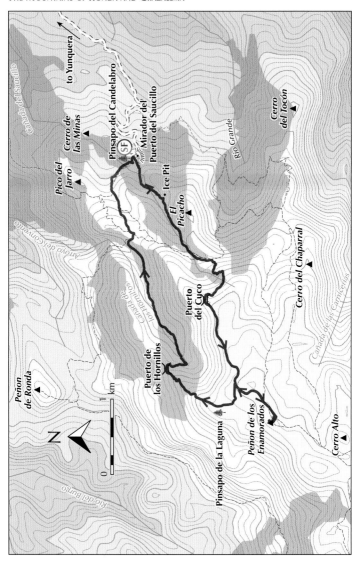

a short diversion to your left to see the old **ice pit** (See Walk 22).

The path climbs parallel to the left bank of the **Cañada del Saucillo**, passing the spring of Fuente de la Perdiz (which is often dry). ▶ Levelling, the path reaches a junction. Keep to your same course following a sign, 'Sendero Puerto Saucillo-Torrecilla' (30min). The Mediterranean and the Sierras de Ojén and Mijas are now visible to the south. Climbing higher past a stand of ancient pinsapos views now open out to the north. Bearing right across an area more denuded of vegetation you reach a divide next to marker posts at the **Puerto del Cuco** (1hr 10min).

Views open out back to the east to the distant peaks of the Sierra Nevada.

Some 100m beyond the Puerto del Cuco the path passes a small, fenced enclosure as you climb gently along the northern side of an exposed ridge: winds can be strong here in winter. At this stage, looking northwards across the valley of the Cañada de los Hornillos you'll be able to spot the footpath by which you will later return.

The path runs through an area where reafforestation is taking place, the saplings protected by green nylon netting. Angling left then right the path, marked by posts, runs on towards Los Enamorados, which looks slightly

The trig point atop Los Enamorados

The ridge top beyond Los Enamorados

wedding cake-like in form. As you draw parallel to the peak, on its southern side, looking up to the right you'll spot a solitary *quejigo* (gall oak).

Here cut right, away from the footpath, at a cairn then passing close to the oak follow a line of cairns up via a low saddle to reach the highest point of **Los Enamorados** (1775m) (2hr).

A vast panorama opens out from **Los Enamorados**, encompassing the Sierra Nevada, the Sierras of Mías, Ojén and Grazalema and out to La Torrecilla, the park's highest peak. From the summit, looking down to the northeast, you'll see a solitary pinsapo: El Pinsapo de la Laguna. Note that you'll be passing it later in the walk.

From the summit head back down to the footpath, then turning left retrace your footsteps back east. Reaching the reafforested area the path angles left then right. Reaching the second of two PR marker posts and a cairn, where to your left you'll see a denuded area among the gorse, cut left towards the solitary pinsapo you could see from Los Enamorados.

The path becomes clearer as it bears right then passes 20m to the right of the **Pinsapo de la Laguna**. Some 125m beyond the pinsapo you reach a large cairn where you should maintain your course. The path begins to descend. Reaching an outcrop of rock, and angling down to the right, the path becomes less distinct. Angling back left it again becomes easier to follow, now sticking close to a descending ridgetop.

After passing to the ridge's northern side a path runs up to merge with yours. Here maintain your course. After looping left and right the path returns to the top of the ridge. Reaching a jagged outcrop of rock you come to a junction at **Puerto de los Hornillos** (2hr 50min).

Here bear right and downwards. Entering a thick stand of pinsapos the path angles left and adopts an easterly course parallel to the stream bed of the **Cañada de los Hornillos**. The path is more overgrown at this point.

After switching back and forth across the stream bed the path bears up and away from its right bank. At a point where another path runs up to meet with yours, cut right and climb steeply away from the valley floor. After passing through a dense stand of ghost-like cedar trees you reach a junction marked by a cairn and a marker post. Turn left (3hr 35min). Passing a marker post you reach another junction. Bearing right between two cairns follow the path down through a mixed stand of pinsapos and Mediterranean pines. Reaching a junction and a marker post turn left. After passing the **Pinsapo del Candelabro**, a Spanish fir with a candelabra-like form, you return to **Puerto del Saucillo** (4hr).

WALK 3
Los Sauces circuit via La Cueva del Agua

Start/Finish	Área Recreativa Los Sauces, 11km from El Burgo
Distance	14.7km
Ascent/Descent	800m
Grade	Medium/Difficult
Time	4hr 15min
Refreshments	None en route
Access	Arriving in El Burgo from Ronda follow the A-366 through the village towards Alozaina. After 1.5km turn right at a sign for 'Los Sauces 9.6km'. Follow the signposted route along forestry tracks to the parking area of Los Sauces.

This remote circuit more than merits its slightly tricky access which entails a drive of 9km along a forestry track to reach Los Sauces, the walk's start point. From this hauntingly beautiful camp ground you first follow a narrow path which rollercoasters through some of the park's most stunning terrain.

A short section of forestry track then leads up to La Cueva del Agua, from where you're minutes away from a high, rocky promontory: it's an ideal picnic spot coming just about halfway through the walk. From here you descend beneath a towering cliff face through an ancient stand of pinsapos into the valley of La Cañada de la Encina from where you follow a slightly overgrown footpath to the isolated farmstead of Cortijo Huarte. Beyond the farm a broad track leads back in a series of lazy loops to Los Sauces.

The walk begins next to a 'P' for parking sign (in front of you is a huge oak beside which is a commemorative plaque to Pierre Edmond Boissier) at the camping area of Los Sauces.

The Swiss botanist **Pierre Edmond Boissier** first catalogued the *Abies pinsapo* – often referred to as Spanish fir – in 1838. He first encountered the

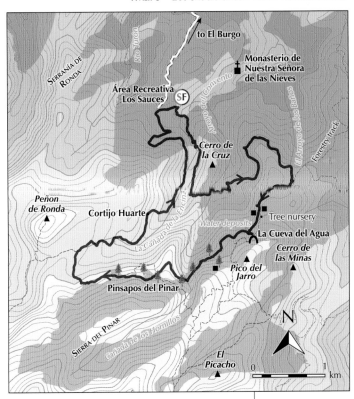

tree in the Sierra Bermeja above Estepona, close to
the Costa del Sol. The pinsapo is found in only four
mountainous areas of southern Spain and two in
the north of Morocco. The trees favour north-facing
slopes between 1500m and 1900m in height with
mild yet wet climatic conditions.

With your back to the 'P' sign bear left past a signboard for Zona de Acampada Controlada Los Sauces.
Descending past a chain blocking vehicle access follow an indistinct track that arcs left to reach an old *era*

(threshing floor). Cut right through a gap in a wall next to the campsite's shower block then descend 30m to a clear footpath. Bearing left, follow the path through a gap in a poled fence beyond which you pass a sign, 'Fin de Sendero', now following GR243 waymarking. After crossing a first stream bed the path bears right following the course of **La Cañada de la Encina**.

Switching from bank to bank the path gently climbs, passing the entrance of a mine shaft.

> **Lead, zinc and silver** were all mined in the Sierra de las Nieves in the early 19th century. The high cost of transporting the minerals out from the mountains lead to their being abandoned by the 1860s.

After running close to the stream's left bank the path angles left then climbs in a series of sharp loops before resuming its former course. After passing the entrance to another mine the path loops more steeply upwards before crossing a rise marked by a cairn and a GR243 marker post.

Descending for a short distance the path bears right then contours round the upper reaches of the valley of the

The convent of Nuestra Señora de las Nieves

Arroyo del Convento through a stand of Mediterranean pines interspersed with a few pinsapos. After crossing two stream beds the **Monasterio de Nuestra Señora de las Nieves** comes into view, down to your left. Climbing once more you now cross a second pass where the trees thin out as views open up to the north and the monastery once more comes into view.

Beyond the pass the path bears sharply right and loops downwards. Contouring round the mountainside, at first on an easterly course, the path bears gradually right to adopt a southerly course. After crossing a fire-break then an area where reafforestation is taking place the path angles in towards **El Arroyo de los Baños** which it soon crosses. Just beyond the stream you reach a **forestry track** and a sign for 'Los Sauces, 4.6km' pointing back along the path you've just walked (1hr 20min).

Here turn right. The track runs gradually uphill, parallel to a ridge to your right. Reaching a small green and yellow sign to your right, it's worth cutting up right for just 75m to the edge of a ridge from where there are vast views to the north. Retrace your steps back to the main path.

The track passes between the fenced buildings of a forestry commission **tree nursery** then after 300m ends next to twin **water deposits**. Immediately beyond the first water deposit cut left and follow an indistinct path steeply upwards to reach a more clearly defined path that bears left up to **La Cueva del Agua** which is flanked by twin pinsapos (1hr 40min). Above the cave is a second deep cleft in the mountainside.

> In spite of its impressive entrance **La Cueva del Agua** is only a few metres deep. Its blackened roof bears witness to the fires that were lit by shepherds who used the cave as shelter for their flocks of sheep and goats.

Leaving La Cueva del Agua drop down for 5m then, bearing left, follow a narrow path that heads down across the hillside to meet with another that runs up from the water deposit next to a GR marker post. Cutting left for

La Cueva del Agua

This is a spectacular place to take a break. Be aware that there are sheer drops immediately in front of the rocks.

225m, you reach a fork. Ignoring GR waymarking that leads up left, maintain your course on the lower, right-hand path. After 75m you pass a small spring which is often dry.

The path climbs as views open out north towards El Burgo before reaching a rocky promontory above a sheer cliff face (2h). ◀

Bearing left and continuing to contour round the mountainside you enter another stand of pinsapos, the **Pinsapos del Pinar**. After climbing, the path descends beneath the rocky crags of the northern face of the **Sierra del Pinar** where the going becomes looser underfoot. After crossing two stream beds the path angles gently upwards before crossing a rise and bearing left reaches more open ground. Some 325m beyond the ridge you reach a fork.

Take the left-hand fork which leads on upwards, re-entering another dense stand of pinsapos. Reaching the next junction, marked by twin cairns, turn right. The path at first climbs in a westerly direction, then after running high above the valley bears right before descending in a series of loops. You reach an area where the dead trunks of pinsapos, some still standing, bear witness to a forest fire of some five years past. The **Peñon de Ronda** (1299m) comes into view to the northwest.

The path levels again, then passing through another thick stand of pinsapos reaches a junction. Take the right-hand fork and descend towards the valley floor as pinsapos give way to Mediterranean pines. Reaching a fire break maintain your course, ignoring a less distinct path that angles right. Your path is marked by cairns and shortly leads to another junction.

Bear right along a sandy footpath that descends in an easterly direction through low-growing pines, lavender and gorse. Ignore any less clearly defined paths that cut left or right. The path, overgrown in parts, eventually loops more steeply downwards, eroded at this stage, as you pass beneath a rocky outcrop then cross the stream bed of **La Cañada de la Encina**.

After running along the stream's left bank, where gorse has taken a hold, the path gradually angles away from the stream, becoming clearer, before leading you round the rickety perimeter fence of **Cortijo Huarte**, a small farmstead built up against a huge boulder (3hr 35min).

Sticking close to the farm's fence the path drops steeply down through pines to reach an open area among trees. Bearing left along the opening's eastern side the path shortly meets with a broad forestry track. ▶ After climbing parallel to La Cañada de la Encina you pass a chain preventing vehicle access then a quarried area to your left.

At a point where the track bears hard left Los Sauces comes into sight. Continue along the track which, bearing once more hard right, descends in a series of loops (which can be shortened by cutting corners on looser, steeper paths) then leads back to **Los Sauces** and your point of departure (4hr 15min).

On the other side of the valley you'll now spot the path you followed earlier in the walk.

WALK 4

*El Burgo circuit via
Puerto de la Mujer*

Start/Finish	Twin signboards beside the Río del Burgo, just outside El Burgo
Distance	14km
Ascent/Descent	375m
Grade	Medium
Time	3hr 45min
Refreshments	None en route
Access	Arriving in El Burgo from Ronda follow the A-366 through the village. Immediately after crossing the bridge over El Río del Burgo turn right at a sign for Senderos. The walk begins at twin signboards to the left of the track after 250m.

This walk provides a fine introduction to the varied terrain of the northern reaches of the Sierra de las Nieves and begins close to the pretty village of El Burgo. After a steep climb up and over Puerto de los Lobos a narrow path leads down to the picnic area at La Fuensanta. From here you follow broad forestry tracks up to a second pass, Puerto de la Mujer. The walk now takes on a livelier tempo as you follow a stunning ridgetop path where views open out to the northwest and southeast.

The road journey from Ronda to El Burgo, and the walk's start point, is an adventure in its own right, leading you through one of Andalucía's wildest expanses of mountain terrain.

The route begins next to twin signboards; one marked 'El Burgo-La Fuensanta', the other 'El Burgo-El Puerto de la Mujer'. From here follow a concrete track whose surface turns to dirt as it climbs between olive groves. Reaching a junction take the right fork along a narrow path, following a sign for 'Yunquera/Los Sauces 9kms'. After 350m you reach another junction. Take the left fork signed for

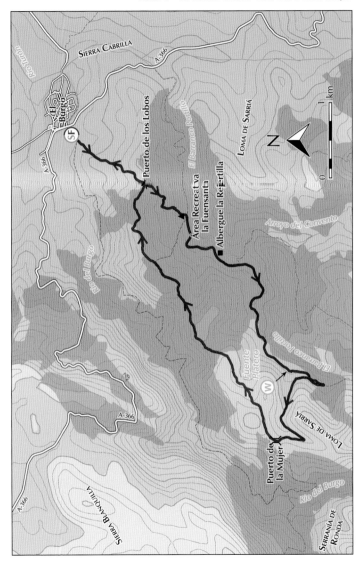

Farm track leaving El Burgo

Views open out eastwards to the Sierra de Cabrilla and south towards the higher peaks of the Sierra de las Nieves.

Área Recreativa la Fuensanta which leads you over the pass of **Puerto de los Lobos**.

From here follow a narrow path marked by cairns and marker posts down through a stand of pine trees. ◄ Passing right of a concrete hut daubed in graffiti you reach a forestry track just to the right of the **Área Recreativa la Fuensanta** (45min).

Here turn right past a stone monument of Christ on the cross, following a sign for Área Recreativa los Sauces. The track climbs gently, following the course of the stream bed of **Barranco de Portillo**. At a point where the track bears right, ignore a track that cuts in to the left across a bridge towards **Albergue la Rejertilla** but rather stick to the main track which runs on close to the edge of Barranco de Portillo. At a point where the road angles left you pass by the **Fuente Platero**. Passing a second stone cross you reach a junction (1hr 40min).

Here turn right following a sign, 'El Burgo/Puerto de la Mujer'. As you follow the track upwards keep an eye open for a fine example of witch's broom in one of the pine trees just to the right of the track.

Witch's broom, also known as bunch disorder, is a common term for an abnormal tree growth caused by the action of an agent such as a virus, an insect, fungus or occasionally mistletoe. This causes dense clusters of shoots to grow out from a single point, resulting in a ball that often has the appearance of a nest or broom. Several plant species can have a witch's broom deformity, including a number of pines.

The path winds hard to the left before passing beneath a power line then cuts once more back to the right before leading up to **Puerto de la Mujer**, marked by a stone and ceramic sign (2hr 20min).

Here leave the track, passing just right of the sign, along a narrow, waymarked path which sticks close to a ridgetop, at first running towards the Sierra Cabrilla. After crossing a fire break it re-enters pine forest. Descending steeply the path crosses a stream bed then climbs and crosses another fire break before resuming its course

The ridgetop path beyond Puerto de la Mujer

along the ridge top, high above the valley of the Río del Burgo. The path crosses a third fire break then a fourth where it angles hard left.

After running towards a rocky outcrop that faces out towards the **Río del Burgo** the path runs along the southeastern side of the ridge where sections are flanked in agave. Crossing back to the other side of the ridge, El Burgo comes into sight as the path leads you back to the junction below **Puerto de los Lobos**. Turn left and retrace your steps back to the start point of the walk (3hr 45min).

EL BURGO

The village has seen settlement since Roman times when it lay on the route between Acinipo, the main Roman settlement in the Ronda mountains, and Málaga. It takes its name from the Moorish period when it was called El Borch. For a brief period it was to come under the sway of the rebel leader Omar Ben Hafsun when he vied for power with the great Caliphate of Córdoba.

The village remained an isolated mountain community for several centuries with an economy based almost exclusively on the production of cereals, grapes, olives and almonds. This was to change in the last century when the arrival of motorised transport linked the town with Ronda and Málaga while the recent arrival of rural tourism, along with the creation of the Natural Park, has brought a steady flow of visitors.

WALK 5

*La Torrecilla circuit via
Puerto de los Pilones*

Start/Finish	Área Recreativa de los Quejigales
Distance	15.7km
Ascent/Descent	975m
Grade	Difficult
Time	5hr 15min or 2hr 35min (omitting La Torrecilla)
Refreshments	None en route
Access	From Ronda take the A-397 towards San Pedro. Shortly after passing a petrol station turn left at a sign for Área Recreativa las Conejeras. Follow a track, which switches between dirt and asphalt, for 9.5km to the Área Recreativa de los Quejigales and a car parking area. Between June and mid-October a barrier blocks vehicle access after 6.7km, adding an extra 2.8km to and from the start point.

La Torrecilla, the highest peak in western Andalucía, numbers among Spain's most spectacular natural viewing points. Towering 1919m above the Mediterranean it looks south to Africa, west to the Atlantic and way out east to the Sierra Nevada.

This challenging walk has the added bonus of passing through one of Europe's few stands of Spanish firs (*Abies pinsapo*) as well as leading you through a magnificent stand of gall oaks on your approach to the summit.

Bear in mind that if you're arriving from Ronda you'll need the best part of an hour to reach the walk's start point even though you have just a little more than 20km to cover.

The walk begins at the entrance to the parking area of Los Quejigales next to a signboard marked 'Área Recreativa' and a map of the park. With your back to the sign turn left following a sign for 'Sendero QuejigalesTorrecilla

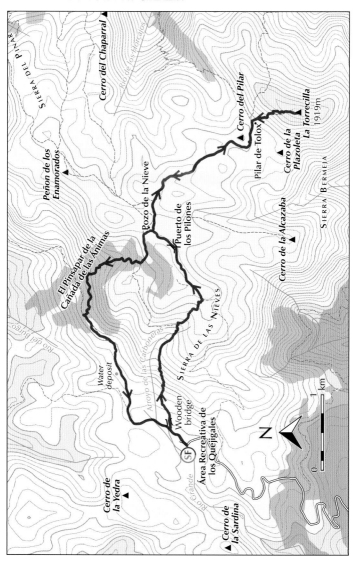

300m'. Passing right of a white hut continue on past a chain across the track then after 200m cut right at a sign for 'QuejigalesTorrecilla 7.2km' and cross a **wooden bridge** via a path that threads upwards, marked by green and white marker posts. Passing a signboard about La Cabra Montés (ibex) the path runs towards a cliff face where it angles left and climbs through the first stand of Spanish firs.

PINSAPOS

The pinsapos of the Cañada del Cuerno are among the oldest found in the park. Before they were protected by law their number had been severely reduced. Many trees were cut down at the time of the construction of the Armada in the 16th century and the population suffered due to both ship-building and charcoal burning, despite being a difficult wood for carpenters to work and a poor source of charcoal. Forest fires, heavy snowfalls and overgrazing further reduced numbers while a latter-day trend to decorate homes with a pinsapo at Christmas – initiated when the Ronda town hall began the practice of decorating the town centre with a huge tree cut down in the Sierra – also took its toll.

As you climb steeply, the Sierra de Grazalema comes into sight to your west. After running close to the stream bed of the **Arroyo de las Carboneras** you reach a marker post and a fork where a line of stones blocks the left-hand path. Bear right and continue to climb. ▸

As you leave the tree line Ronda comes into view and, far beyond, Olvera.

The path leads on through an area where young saplings have been replanted to reach a forestry track. Turn left following a sign, 'Sendero QuejigalesTorrecilla'. The track runs towards an antenna as vast views open out southwards to the coast and the Mediterranean, shortly reaching the flat ridge top of **Puerto de los Pilones** (1750m). Ignoring a track leading up to the antenna bear right along a narrow path that passes through more replanted saplings. The path crosses a stream bed, shored up against erosion, before running on through an area of deciduous oaks: a signboard tells you about this Quejigal de Alta Montaña, or stand of Portuguese oaks.

OAKS

Quercus faginea, or Portuguese oak, is one of a handful of oaks native to the Iberian peninsula. The trees can live to well over 100 years and can grow up to 20m in height. The tree often develops oak galls, which are formed by gall wasps laying eggs in the bark of young branches. The gall wasp larva grows inside the gall until it is able to bore its way out via the small hole that you see on all galls.

Extensive stands of gall and holm oaks were worked over the centuries by *carboneros* (charcoal burners) at a time when the fuel was used to heat homes throughout the region. The Sierra's extensive stands of forest also provided a rich source of timber for a ship-building industry that thrived along both the Mediterranean and Atlantic seaboards until the advent of iron and steel-built ships. Charcoal burning, which continued in the area until some 50 years back, devastated the original oak forest in the Sierra de las Nieves.

You could shorten the walk by about 2 hours and avoid a final steep climb by cutting left here.

The path runs down to reach a flat area where, just to your left, is a recently restored ice pit or **Pozo de Nieve** (1hr 25min). ◄

The numerous *pozos de hielo* (**ice pits**) throughout the Sierra bear witness to an age when ice was a much-prized commodity throughout Andalucía. Winter snows were trampled underfoot to make ice within walled pits which were then covered with earth and branches to slow down the melting process. The ice was later wrapped in thick sacking, laden on mules and distributed as far away as Cádiz and Sevilla.

If climbing La Torrecilla, bear right. Descending gently you reach a junction where a sign points left for Puerto del Saucillo. Ignoring this footpath bear right following waymarking for PRA-351. The footpath runs across flatter, grassy pockets between the jagged limestone. Out to the east the Sierra Nevada and Sierra de la Contraviesa are visible on clear days while to the south the Moroccan Rif mountains can sometimes be seen. The path runs on through an area where more reafforestation is taking place, adopting a course running almost due south towards La Torrecilla.

Angling right the path passes between the rocky outcrop of the **Cerro del Pilar** (1761m) and the Cerro de la Plazoleta. Dropping down past a small shrine in the rocks the path reaches the beautifully carved troughs at the **Pilar de Tolox**.

> The carved blocks of limestone of the **Pilar de Tolox**, also marked on some maps as La Fuente de los Machos, almost certainly date back to Roman times. During that period the Sierra de las Nieves provided summer grazing for the flocks from the lower pastures close to Málaga and the Bay of Algeciras. Some of the walks in the park follow the ancient transhumance routes that lead up into the park.

The Pilar de Tolox

The cairn at La Torrecilla's summit at 1919m

Just beyond the troughs, reaching the base of La Torrecilla, the path bears right before looping up in a series of zigzags to the highest point of the Sierra de la Nieves, **La Torrecilla** (1919m) (2hr 55min).

On a clear day from the summit of **La Torrecilla** all of western Andalucía's principal landmarks are visible: La Sierra del Pinar, La Sierra Bermeja, Gibraltar, the Moroccan Rif, La Concha, La Sierra de Mijas, La Maroma, La Sierra de Contraviesa, La Sierra Nevada and El Torcal de Antequera, as well as a large number of *Pueblos Blancos* (White Villages) and coastal settlements.

From here retrace your steps back to the flat area surrounding the Pozo de la Nieve (4hr 5min). Cut right, passing close to the ice pit, and continue to the far end of a flat area among the rocks. Climbing up across the rocks to the top of a low ridge you reach a trig point. Bear left across more open ground where, descending once more, pinsapos reappear before you reach a junction marked by three large cairns.

Here, cutting right, you enter a thicker stand of Spanish firs, **El Pinsapar de la Cañada de las Ánimas**. After following the path, marked clearly with cairns, steeply downwards you'll spot a more open area to your right where vast views open out towards the northern reaches of the Sierra de las Nieves, while to your left a jagged ridge-line towers above you. ▶

Views to the west on the final descent through the pinsapo forest

This is a great spot to break for a rest.

Continuing down the footpath the pinsapos thin out as views open out as you cross a more open swathe of mountainside dotted with hawthorn, before the path leads across two gullies, shored up with wired retaining walls. The path broadens to become wide enough for vehicle access, leading on past a **water deposit** as you cut through an area where reafforestation is underway. Descending, another track runs in from the right to merge with yours. Maintaining your course you pass the **wooden bridge** you crossed earlier in the walk then arrive back at your point of departure (5hr 15min).

WALK 6

Ronda Gorge circuit

Start/Finish	Parador on the western side of the Puente Nuevo in Ronda
Distance	6km
Ascent/Descent	240m
Grade	Easy/Medium
Time	1hr 40min
Refreshments	None en route

This short circuit out from Ronda gets you up close to the dramatic cliffs and spectacular gorge and bridge whose beauty have made the town one of Europe's most popular tourist destinations.

After leaving the town along a sandy footpath that runs close to the cliff's edge you follow a winding country lane across the bowl of the valley past numerous smallholdings and country houses before climbing steeply back up to the town's historical centre via a cobbled footpath that hugs the gorge's spectacular eastern flank. From here you're treated to mesmerising views of the town's famous bridge, the Puente Nuevo, and El Tajo (the gorge).

The walk begins in front of the Parador, on the western side of the Puente Nuevo. With your back to the Parador turn left and leave the square along a pedestrianised street, Calle José Aparicio. At the end of the street turn left again. Passing the bullring you reach busts of Orson Welles and Ernest Hemingway. Cut right along the Paseo de Orson Welles. Passing in front of Ronda's ugly municipal theatre you reach the small park of La Alameda.

Orson Welles and Ernest Hemingway were both frequent visitors to Ronda during the late 50s and early 60s at a time when both struck up a lasting friendship with the bullfighter Antonio Ordoñez. Two years after his death Welles' ashes were

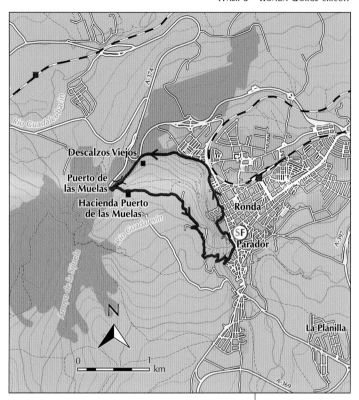

scattered at the Recreo de San Cayetano, a farm belonging to the Ordoñez family, just to the north of Ronda. Hemingway had the Ronda bridge in mind when describing a battle in his novel *For Whom the Bell Tolls* even though the book depicts fighting along the Aragonese front.

Cut right along the park's central walkway then reaching a statue of Pedro Romero bear right and exit the park. Turn left then passing right of the Iglesia de la Merced, continue along Calle Jerez. After passing Hotel

Reina Victoria the street angles right past a statue of the Virgen del Rocío then once more left before reaching a roundabout. Keep left, sticking close to the cliff edge, which is just to your left.

After some 200m bear left, away from the road, along a dirt track following a sign for Bodega Descalzos Viejos. Running close to a wall topped by a fence, the surface of the track changes to tarmac as it leads you past the entrance gate to **Descalzos Viejos**.

> The exquisitely beautiful 16th-century monastery of **Descalzos Viejos** – the Discalced Order of Trinitarian Monks – is now home to one of the Ronda region's top *bodegas* (wineries) and one of the few that offers tours and tastings. The main winery is housed within the chapel where murals were discovered depicting Santa Justa and Santa Rufina, the patron saints of Seville. Tastings, combined with tapas, can be arranged. Call Flavio Salesi 607 167482 www.descalzosviejos.com

The ridgetop beyond Descalzos Viejos

Continue on your same course along a sandy track which, passing a green gate, narrows to become a footpath that runs gently downhill, close to the edge of the cliff, at first parallel to a stone wall. Angling right the footpath drops down to meet with a tarmac road. Turn left following a sign, 'Ronda GR141, GR249'. Passing through a breach in the mountain (35min), **Puerto de las Muelas**, the road cuts left before descending towards the valley floor. Reaching the gates of **Hacienda Puerto de las Muelas** bear left following a sign for Haza del Batán and follow a winding lane on past the gates of Haza del Batán where twin statues of Christ on the cross and the Virgin are enclosed in a glass case.

Descending through groves of olive and walnut trees you reach a fork. Take the right-hand option. Reaching gates marked '21' the lane descends, closer now to Ronda's majestic south-facing cliff face. Crossing a bridge over the **Río Guadalevín** the road angles to the right and climbs steeply. Angling once more left it descends to reach a junction with a cobbled track (1hr). Turn right and climb up past a building marked 'Molinos del Tajo'.

After passing twin signs for Albergue Los Molinos the track reaches a second set of signs for La Hoya del Tajo, one depicting the birds that can be seen in the gorge. Leave the track here and follow a narrow path which climbs steeply up the eastern side of the Ronda gorge before passing through a narrow opening in the wall that in Moorish times served as Ronda's lower line of defence. ▸

Beyond the gap you're treated to a stunning view of the Puente Nuevo that spans the gorge.

The **Ronda gorge**, plunging to 120m at its deepest point, was formed over many millennia by the gradual attrition of the River Guadalevín.

The bridge which spans the gorge, the **Puente Nuevo**, was completed in 1793. It replaced a previous single span bridge which collapsed in 1741 killing 50 people. The bridge's massive supporting columns reflect a desire to ensure such a disaster would never reoccur.

The approach to the Puente Nuevo in summer

Angling right head on up a path parallel to the wall, then go left up a flight of steps and follow a path that zigzags steeply up to reach Ronda's historic quarter and the Plaza María Auxiladora. Turn left and exit the square along Calle Tenorio. After passing Casa Don Bosco you reach another small square. Pass left of three wrought iron benches to reach a junction and a ceramic mural, Ronda y Los Viajeros Románticos. Turning left, and crossing the Puente Nuevo, you return to the start point of the walk (1hr 40min).

WALK 7

*Ronda to the Tajo del Abanico and
the Virgen de la Cabeza chapel*

Start/Finish	La Puerta de Almocábar, Ronda
Distance	14km
Ascent/Descent	375m
Grade	Medium
Time	3hr 35min (or 2hr 20min to the cave and back; 1hr 35min to the chapel and back)
Refreshments	None en route

Ronda's gorge, known to locals simply as El Tajo is what most visitors to the town remember best. Yet it's eclipsed by another hidden gorge which lies just a few kilometres from the town: the Tajo del Abanico or the Gorge of the Fan. It takes its name from the shape of the cave entrance that you pass as you thread your way southwards between towering sandstone cliffs by way of a stunning medieval footpath. This route make a detour on its return leg to visit the beautiful mountain chapel of the Virgen de la Cabeza where every spring a *romería* (country festivity) takes place, one of the city's most colourful feast days.

The walk begins in front of the Almocábar gate at the eastern end of Ronda's old town next to a spring. With your back to the spring turn right, cross a zebra crossing, then follow the A-369 passing just left of the Bodega de San Francisco. After 250m just as you pass house number 20 go right, up a cobbled street which climbs past the water channel leading to **El Predicatorio**. ▸

The Victorian traveller and artist **David Roberts** painted a landscape of the city from this spot.

El Predicatorio, possibly of Roman origin, was part of an elaborate water system that brought water to Ronda's old town from a spring to the east of the city. Open air masses were once held here, thus its name, 'the place of sermons'.

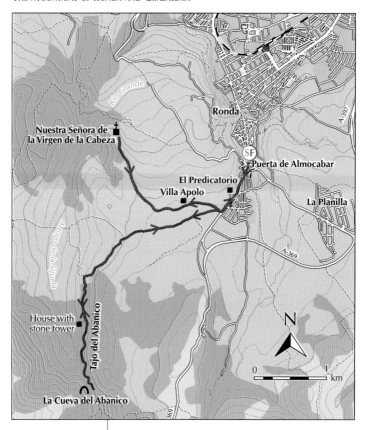

The street merges once more with the **A-369**. Continue straight ahead at a mini roundabout then after 100m go right at a sign for Ermita Rupestre Virgen de la Cabeza. After 35m, reaching a fork (10min), bear left past a 30km speed limit sign then follow a tarmac road that runs between olive groves. Soon you pass the entrance gates to La Hoya de los Frailes.

Reaching a fork (30min) keep left, following a blue arrow on a rock and GR141 waymarking. Passing twin

sets of black metal gates the gorge begins to narrow down, with towering cliffs to your left. You pass a **house with a stone tower** at its southern end, the entrance gates of Huerta de la Cazalla.

The valley of El Tajo del Abanico

Just before the track cuts right towards a gate with a plaque depicting the Virgin, cut left on a path that passes through a metal gate marked **Tajo del Abanico**. The footpath threads its way through evergreen oaks before passing an old threshing platform with a sign for Punto de Observación Astronómico. The path arcs left, now beautifully surfaced in ancient herring-bone cobbles, then passing through a metal gate descends to the floor of the gorge where you cross the oleander-lined stream bed of the **Arroyo de la Sijuela**.

Although some sources claim that the **cobbled footpath** is Roman in origin, its intricate cobbling almost certainly dates from the medieval period. The path was once part of the drovers' path that linked the villages of the Genal valley to the market town of Ronda.

75

Beyond the stream you pass beneath the fan-shaped cave that gives the gorge its name, **La Cueva del Abanico** (1hr 20min).

Passing the cave the path again becomes cobbled before it reaches another gate. Retrace your footsteps to the junction you reached at 10min (2hr 10min). You can turn right here and retrace your footsteps back to the walk's start point or continue to the chapel of the Virgen de la Cabeza.

Optional extension to the chapel of the Virgen de la Cabeza

If you wish to visit the chapel of the Virgen de la Cabeza turn left. Shortly to your right you will see a house with a tower, the **Villa Apolo**, which was severely damaged during the Civil War. The track passes a white house with three palm trees as the track's concrete surface turns to dirt. Levelling, the track passes a row of umbrella pines. Just before you reach a gate marked 'Camino Privado' head right, down a steep cobbled track to reach the mountain chapel of **Nuestra Señora de la Virgen de la Cabeza** (2hr 45min).

> The chapel of **Nuestra Señora de la Virgen de la Cabeza** is of Mozarabic origin (Mozarabs were Christian inhabitants living in Spain during the Moorish period). It numbers among the oldest Christian places of worship in Spain, dating back to the 9th and 10th centuries. A colourful romería takes place at the chapel every year in July when the Virgen de la Cabeza is carried from the old town of Ronda, and an open air mass is celebrated in her honour.

From here retrace your footsteps back to the start point of the walk (3hr 35min).

WALK 8
Ronda Old Town historical circuit

Start/Finish	Parador on the western side of the Puente Nuevo, Ronda
Distance	4.5km
Ascent/Descent	125m
Grade	Easy
Time	1hr 30min
Refreshments	There are a number of springs/drinking fountains as well as bars and shops.

Ronda's old town centre is divided into three distinct areas. La Ciudad corresponds to what was once the old Moorish citadel. El Mercadillo, just to its west, developed once the Puente Nuevo had been built and is now the town's commercial centre. The Barrio de San Francisco, just east of the old town walls, dates from medieval times when a souk or market sprung up outside the old city walls and which, with time, developed into a flourishing quarter of the city.

This serpentine walking tour introduces you to the three areas' most beautiful back streets and monuments. Timings quoted are for walking the circuit without stopping to visit individual buildings: if you plan to do so the walk could easily become a four to five-hour circuit. It's worth dropping into the Ronda Tourist Office, which you pass at the beginning of the walk, to pick up a town map as well as a list of opening times for the different sites and museums. This old town walk is best saved for the afternoon: from around 10am until 4pm the town is often swamped by tour groups on coach trips up from the Costa del Sol.

RONDA

The high plateau on which Ronda now sits has seen human presence since Neolithic times and in all likelihood long before that: the troglodytes who painted symbols and animals in the Pileta cave (see Walk 13) during the Palaeolithic period would almost certainly have looked out from this extraordinary natural observatory. The Romans built an important urbis which they knew as Arunda – from which the town takes its name – while the Visigoths continued to occupy the town. They built one of Spain's earliest Christian churches on a hillside just south of the town (Walk 7 takes you to this exceptionally beautiful chapel).

It was during the time of the Moors that the town began to take on its present day appearance: a sizeable slice of its original fortifications bears witness to their presence as does the extraordinary subterranean passage of La Mina. Ronda became a key settlement on Granada's western frontier and only fell to the Christians in 1485. Much of the town east of the gorge was built on the foundations of the Moorish settlement with the mosque's minaret being reinvented as a belfry to the town's cathedral.

The town only saw westward expansion once the Puente Nuevo was completed. That same decade saw the opening of its most famous civic building, La Plaza de Toros, where the rules of the modern bullfight were laid down and where the Romero and Ordoñez dynasties made the town synonymous with the fighting of bulls or *tauromaquía*.

The walk begins in front of the Parador on the western side of the Puente Nuevo. With your back to the Parador turn left and leave the square along a pedestrianised street, Calle José Aparicio. At the end of the street turn left again. Passing between the Ronda Tourist Office and the **bullring** continue along a path flanked by busts of Orson Welles and Ernest Hemingway. Take the next path to your left past a plaque dedicated to the Japanese artist Miki Haruta then go right to reach a bandstand and a stunning **balcony** which overhangs the cliff edge.

Retrace your footsteps back to the busts then turn left along a marble flagged walkway, El Paseo de Orson Welles. Reaching the gardens of **La Alameda** head left to a series of cliffside **balconies** from where you are treated to more panoramic views of the mountains to the south and west of Ronda.

With your back to the cliff edge follow the central thoroughfare through the gardens to reach a statue of Pedro Romero. Angle right, exit the gardens then bearing

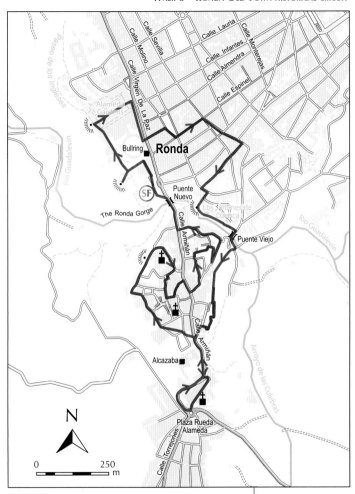

once more right continue along **Calle Virgen de la Paz** to the north side of the **Plaza de Toros** (bullring) where you reach the statues of the bullfighters Antonio Ordoñez and Cayetano Ordoñez. Cross the street to the post office, turn right then reaching the Unicaja bank cut left along Calle Pedro Romero to reach La Plaza del Socorro.

> **Pedro Romero** numbers among Spain's most famous bullfighters. He fought more than 500 bulls without ever being gored or suffering serious injury and killed his last bull when aged 77. Ronda's annual *feria* is named in his honour – La Feria de Pedro Romero. It culminates with a bullfight in the same ring where Romero perfected his fighting style.

To your left, beyond a statue of Blas Infante, is the old Ronda casino (in Spain the term equates more closely to a gentleman's club rather than a place to gamble). Ahead of you, beyond a statue of Hercules, is La Iglesia del Socorro.

Head right across the square, then cut left up Ronda's main pedestrianised shopping street, **Calle Espinel**, known to all locals as La Calle de la Bola.

> **La Calle de la Bola** literally means The Street of the Ball. The origin of the name, according to most sources, dates from the year when a group of children created a huge snowball in the street following a heavy snowfall. Exceptionally low temperatures that winter ensured that the snowball remained at one end of the street for several weeks. Other sources claim that it take its name from a children's game similar to marbles that was once played in the street.

Taking the next turning right you reach the square of Plaza Carmen Abela. Head along the left side of the square and continue down Calle Santa Cecilia, passing right of El Temple de los Horcados then after 15m cut right along Calle Yeseros. At the end of this narrow street you pass by La Posada de las Ánimas. Head straight on along Calle Cerrillo then, reaching the end of the street, descend a flight of steps then turn left and after 30m angle right along Calle de la Mina. Follow the street as it arcs left then turn right through a metal gate to reach **Los Jardines de Cuenca**.

Here, cutting down steps to your right, you reach a **viewpoint** from where you have a stunning view of the gorge and the **Puente Nuevo**. From here follow the gardens' lower wall, descending several flights of steps, to reach the bottom gate of the gardens. Leaving the gardens cut right and drop down several flights of steps. ▶ Cut right across the **Puente Viejo** from where, further down the gorge, Ronda's oldest bridge, El Puente de San Miguel, is also visible.

To your left you'll see the eight-spouted spring of Ocho Caños and just beyond, La Iglesia de Padre Jesús.

At the far side of the bridge (30min), from where the Arco de Carlos V is visible up ahead, cut left down a flight of steps to reach Los Baños Árabes. From the baths retrace your footsteps back uphill for 35m then cut left and follow a damaged flight of steps up to the Arab battlements that once protected the town's lower, north-eastern flank. Here you enter the Moorish citadel-fortress via a keyhole arched gate, La Puerta de Xijara. Head on between a parallel line of fortifications.

After some 100m a flight of stairs leads up onto the battlements and to a tower from whose roof there are

The church of El Espiritú Santo seen from the Moorish battlements

The northern battlements of the old Moorish citadel

fine views of the Espíritu Santo church to the east. Exit the square at its far end via a flight of steps, just left of a wheelchair ramp, then turn left along Calle Coleta. Reaching **Calle Armiñan**, the road that dissects the old town of Ronda, turn left then after 100m bear left away from the street down a cobbled street that leads down past the **Espíritu Santo church** to reach the town's eastern battlements.

Exiting through La Puerta de Almocábar (55min) you reach Plaza Ruedo Alameda where the town's weekly market was once held. Angle right along the battlements, cross a pedestrian crossing, then follow the road round to the right as it passes beneath the remains of the Moorish Alcazaba. After repeating a 75m section of the route you followed earlier cut left up a flight of stairs at a sign for Ayuntamiento de Ronda to reach Plaza Duquesa de Parcent. ◄

To your immediate right is the Ronda ayuntamiento *(town hall) and, just beyond to its left, La Iglesia de Santa María la Mayor.*

Head straight across the gardens in the middle of the square past a bust of the eponymous Duquesa de Parcent. Reaching Café Mondragón go right, along a narrow street that hugs the southern side of the Convento de la Caridad, leading you past the Palacio de Mondragón. Reaching house number 7 cut left to reach Plaza María Auxiliadora from where there are soaring views out across the bowl of the Ronda valley.

Go right along the edge of the square past the music conservatory, then continue along Calle Tenorio, shortly passing Casa Don Bosco. Reaching a divide in the road go right, past Bar El Nogal, then follow the road as it angles right and passes the church of **Nuestra Señora de la Paz**. At the end of the street turn right along Calle Marqués de Moctezuma then cut left between La Casa del Gigante and Museo Joaquín Peinado. Continue along a narrow cobbled street to reach the back wall of the **Iglesia de Santa María la Mayor**.

Here go left along Calle González Campos. Reaching a small square angle left again in front of house number 13 along another narrow street to return to **Calle Armiñan**. Cross the street and cut right for 50m then reaching Plaza Abul Beka cut left past the Alminar de San Sebastian. Take the first street to the left, Calle Virgen de la Aurora. Take the next turning to the right, descend a flight of steps, then go right for 15m then once more hard left in front of house number 26. Descending Calle Marqués de Salvatierra you reach a small square

The belfry of Santa María, built atop a Moorish minaret

El Puente Nuevo seen from the south

graced by the elegant façade of the Palacio Marqués de Salvatierra.

Here cut left up Calle Cuesta de Santo Domingo passing by the entrance to La Mina then the main entrance to the Palacio del Rey Moro. Continue straight uphill to reach **Calle Armiñan** once again. Bear right past a ceramic mural, Ronda a Los Viajeros Románticos, then the Convento de Santo Domingo. Head straight across the Puente Nuevo to return to your point of departure (1hr 30min).

THE GENAL AND GUADIARO VALLEYS

Coppiced chestnut grove in autumn (Walk 9)

Agave-lined footpath on the ascent back to Alpandeire (Walk 11)

Running on a southeasterly course from the Ronda mountains towards the sea, the Genal and Guadiaro river valleys meet some 10 kilometres south of Gaucín before flowing into the Mediterranean at Nuevo Guadiaro, a few kilometres north of Gibraltar. In spite of their proximity, lying between the Sierra Bermeja to the east and the Grazalema and Alcornocales parks to the west, the two valleys are strikingly different in nature while both are home to some superb walking trails.

The river valley of the Genal is divided between seven villages of the Alto Genal and another eight in the Bajo Genal with a total population that numbers just 7000. If you enjoy getting well off the beaten track, this is the place to do it: it's only in the past 10 years that rural tourism has arrived in the area and an extensive network of PR trails marked out between the villages.

The Guadiaro valley – the river takes its name from the Arabic Wad Auro or River of Gold – lies just a few kilometres west of that of the Genal yet its landscape is quite different, more similar to the limestone scenery that typifies the Grazalema mountains. Cork oaks are also present yet here they are interspersed with large extensions of olive and almond groves along with magnificent old holm oaks. The valley sides are far more rugged and the peaks much higher while weather systems from the Atlantic exert a greater influence than those of the Mediterranean.

The valley has seen greater development than that of the Genal, being of easier access and lying on the main trade route that connected the Ronda mountains and the Campo de Gibraltar: this explains why the area is particularly rich in archaeological remains (see 'Andalucían historical overview' in the Introduction). Yet these villages remained comparatively isolated until the Ronda to Algeciras railway line was opened in the 1890s and a road built along the valley that linked Ronda with Cortes de la Frontera.

If you're staying in Ronda you could travel by train to the start points of Walks 12, 13 and 14 and you could pick up the circuit described in Walk 16 at the point where it passes through Estación de Cortes.

PLANTS AND WILDLIFE

The proximity of the Mediterranean has a notable influence on the climate of the valley with an average annual temperature of 14°C. This mild climate, coupled with abundant rain during the winter months, nurtures remarkably fecund plant life and the Genal valley is home to some of the largest extensions of forest in southern Spain. Most notable are the vast stands of chestnut (*Castanea sativa*) of the Alto Genal which are best seen from November through to mid-December when dressed in their autumnal splendour.

Further south along the valley chestnut forest gives way to stands of cork oak, gall oak and pine. The harvesting of cork replaces that of chestnuts as keystone of the local economy: Walks 17 and 18 both pass through

stands of cork oak (*Quercus suber*) which look particularly striking after the trees have been stripped of their cork, an event which takes place once every 9 to 14 years once the trees have reached around 50 years of age.

Together with walkers, the Genal valley has also recently become a popular destination for the birding community. Breeding birds include griffon and Egyptian vultures, golden, booted, Bonelli's and short-toed eagles, peregrine falcon, lesser kestrel, eagle owl, white-rumped, Alpine and pallid swift, blue rock thrush, rock thrush, black redstart, chough, rock sparrow, rock bunting, black wheatear, crag martin and crossbill. You'll often be treated to the sounds of the woodpecker, nightingale and cuckoo. If you'd like a list of the more common species visit www.cicerone. co.uk/803/resources

The plant and animal life of the Guadiaro valley are very similar to those found in the Grazalema mountains (see the Grazalema general introduction) while the valley is best seen during the Andalucían spring when the wildflowers are at their brilliant best (for a list of the more common species visit www.cicerone. co.uk/803/resources). In winter the valley is spectacular when its many almond trees come into blossom.

VILLAGES

One long, narrow and winding road links the villages of the Alto Genal and gives access to the trailheads of the walks described in this guide. Igualeja is the largest village and it is here that the Genal makes its spectacular *entrée en scène* (Walk 9 leads you to the source of the river). Yet like its near neighbours, the village attracts surprisingly few visitors. Alpandeire and Cartajima, where three of the walks begin, are similarly untouristy and both have decent places to stay (see Appendix C).

The one village that sees much more action is Júzcar, the village that was changed from white to blue for the Sony 2011 *The Smurfs in 3D* film. Oddly and bizarrely blue it remains (read why in Walk 10 which passes through the village).

The villages of the Bajo Genal are generally larger than those at the north of the valley, and of easier

access. Benarrabá, which looks east across the valley, has a small hotel which has long been popular with walking groups (see Appendix C). A few kilometres away, on the other side of the valley, Genalguacíl is unique in having an extraordinary collection of street art as a result of its biannual Encuentros de Arte when artists from throughout Spain gather in the village: you'll see several of these remarkable creations if you tackle Walk 17.

Gaucín, at the west of the Genal valley, has stunning views south to Gibraltar and Morocco. The village has a large ex-pat population which partially explains why the offer of good food and accommodation is more extensive than in other parts of the valley.

Montejaque, the starting point for the beautiful circuit described in

Cartajima backed by the jagged ridge of Los Riscos (Walk 10)

Wildflower explosion beneath the olives (Walk 12)

Walk 19, is the most attractive of *los Pueblos Blancos* (the White Villages) of the Guadiaro valley and could make a great base for a walking holiday in the area. Benaoján, known throughout Andalucía for its hams and charcuterie, is a more workaday village and sees fewer visitors, while a little further south along the valley Jimera de Líbar is one of the region's prettiest and quietest villages with a charming small hotel.

The railside settlement of Estación de Benaoján also has a hotel next to the rushing waters of the Santo stream while Cortes de la Frontera, in spite of it being the largest of the villages along the Guadiaro valley, has no hotel accommodation.

MAPS

The best maps of the area are the three 1:50000 I.N.G quadrants, Ubrique 1050, Marbella 1065 and Cortes de la Frontera 1064.

TAXIS

- Cortes de la Frontera: Juan 600 219 795
- Montejaque: Alonso 607 919 352

WALK 9

*Cartajima eastern circuit via
Parauta and Igualeja*

Start/Finish	Town hall, Cartajima
Distance	15.5km
Ascent/Descent	750m
Grade	Medium/Difficult
Time	4hr 20min
Refreshments	Shops and bars in Parauta and Igualeja
Note	After heavy rain the river crossing can be difficult while at other times you may find it easier to remove boots and socks.

This moderately challenging circuit passes through three of the Genal valley's prettiest villages. The walk is mostly by way of farm tracks that cut through the ancient chestnut groves that are so much a part of the upper Genal's landscape: walking here is particularly memorable when the trees are dressed in their autumnal colours. As you leave Cartajima you're treated to fine views north towards the jagged crest of Los Riscos, one of Andalucía's most striking karst limestone formations.

Be ready for three stiff climbs and bear in mind that if you undertake the walk after heavy rain you may need to remove your boots when you cross the Arroyo de los Granados.

The walk begins in front of the *ayuntamiento* (town hall), just beneath the main entrance of the church of Nuestra Señora del Rosario. With your back to the town hall turn right then right again. Drop down a flight of steps then turn left past a tobacconist's shop. At the first fork keep right. Reaching house number 1 go left and continue along Calle Hacha. At the end of this street, just before reaching recycling bins, bear left at a sign for 'Parauta 1hr 15min' down a broad track.

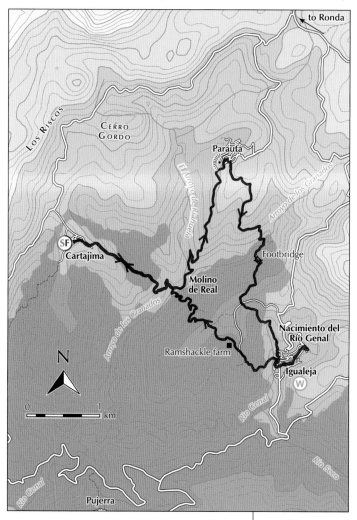

You shortly pass a huge chestnut tree where a sign-board calculates its age to be some 300 years.

The annual **chestnut harvest** forms a vital part of the region's economy, earning local farmers an estimated €10 million per annum. Yet the future of chestnut farming is now in the balance with the recent arrival of the oriental chestnut gall wasp, (*Dryocosmus kuriphilus*), which has already put paid to an estimated 70% of Italy's annual harvest. Its one known predator, the tiny *Torymus sinensis* insect, has recently been released in the area; local producers are anxiously waiting to see what the consequences might be.

Ignoring turnings leading into groves to your right and left follow the main track down to the bottom of the valley (30min) where you cross a tributary of the Genal,

300 year old chestnut tree passed at the beginning of the walk

El Arroyo de Riahuela, then after 90m cross the bed of the **Arroyo de los Granados** via stepping stones. Bearing left you pass by **Molino del Real**.

The track climbs, levels, then angling right then left climbs once again. Reaching a junction follow the way-marked main track which loops hard to the right then once again left. The track sticks close to a ridgetop as it runs on up towards Parauta, and views open out across the valley to Cartajima. After passing the spring of Fuente Nueva you reach the outskirts of **Parauta** where the track passes a mirador and twin benches to reach a three-way divide. Take the middle option and continue just to the right of a metal railing.

Cutting right just past house number 9 you reach the main square of Parauta, La Plaza de la Constitución (1hr 15min). Passing between four benches, cut right up Calle Altillo via a flight of steps. ▸

Following the street to the right then left past a bench, cut left at the end of a metal railing. Angling right you pass house number 32, then angling back left climb steeply via a paved footpath to reach a broad track. Turn right.

Views once more open out towards the west and Cartajima as you follow a concrete track in a southeasterly direction through groves of walnut. After passing beneath power lines concrete gives way to dirt as you cross the stream bed of the **Arroyo de los Granados**. Some 100m beyond the stream you reach a marker post where the track swings hard left towards a metal gate. Maintaining your course across a stream bed then bearing right behind a solitary oak, continue up a narrow track which narrows to become a path as it runs up through chestnut groves towards power lines.

After crossing a stream bed via a wooden-posted **footbridge** the path angles right before assuming its steep ascent. Shortly before reaching a ridgetop the path angles left through a gap in a fence (its wire-and-post gate is normally left open) then crosses the ridge. Passing a brick-posted gate the path widens to become a track which crossing a second ridgetop reaches a four-way junction.

If you exit the square at its far end, just right of house number 6 after a few metres you will reach Bar Anafe, where you could break for alfresco refreshments.

Continue straight ahead, passing between two metal posts.

Igualeja comes into sight as you drop down a concrete track which soon reverts to dirt. After a deeply eroded section the track again becomes concrete as you reach the outskirts of Igualeja where you drop down Calle La Tetona. At the bottom of the street turn right then after 15m go hard left, following metal railings. The street cuts right then back left before descending three cobbled steps to reach a junction and a shop marked 'Tienda' (store). Turn left to reach a square where to your right a balcony offers views down to El Genal. Note that you will later be returning to this spot.

Exit the square past a sign, 'Camino de Ronda'. Bearing right continue down Calle del Canal past a spring to the Plaza del Divino Pastor. Go left along Calle Baja to reach the main square of the village, Plaza Andalucía (2hr 40min). ◄

To your left Restaurante El Perol is a good choice if you plan to break for a drink or a meal.

Exit the square past the Unicaja bank along a narrow street then turn left along Calle Barrero. After passing a church you reach a fountain and a roundabout where you should take the exit to the right. Just before reaching a bridge and a hotel cut right to reach **El Nacimiento del Río Genal**. From here retrace your footsteps back via the Plaza Andalucía then the Plaza del Divino Pastor to the small square with views across the stream bed of the Genal (3hr 10min).

Passing just right of the balcony overlooking the Genal, exit the square the same way you entered earlier in the walk then take the first turning left past house number 5 along a concrete track which climbs, reverts to dirt, then narrows to become a path. Reaching a fork by a house with a narrow bridge leading to its entrance cut right up a narrow path which climbs between steep banks, cobbled in sections.

Eventually, steps cut into a steep bank lead you up to a track. Go left, climb for 50m to reach a junction with a broader track, then turn right. The track's concrete section ends before running up to a fork. Angle left then follow an eroded track down past a **ramshackle farm**. Passing

beneath an overhead power line the track loops steeply up before passing through a breach in the ridgetop to reach a four-way junction.

El Nacimiento (the source) del Río Genal

Go straight ahead, crossing a track that bisects yours, then descend into the next valley. The track becomes concrete then describes a series of lazy loops. Reaching a junction where you'll see a blue No Through Road sign in a tree to your left, go hard right. The track continues to descend, passing a garish blue shed. Looping steeply on down it narrows to become a footpath which after a few metres passes a small white shed.

Some 30m before reaching the Arroyo de los Granados the path angles hard right. Follow it parallel to the river for 75m then go left, cross via stepping stones (or by removing your boots) then cut left up a track and retrace your footsteps back to the start point of the walk (4hr 20min).

WALK 10

Cartajima southern circuit via
Pujerra and Júzcar

Start/Finish	Town hall, Cartajima
Distance	13.5km
Ascent/Descent	800m
Grade	Medium/Difficult
Time	4hr
Refreshments	Bars and shops in Pujerra and Júzcar
Note	You may need to remove footwear when crossing the Río Genal.
Warning	Not recommended after heavy rainfall when the Genal might be in spate.

This superb, moderately challenging circuit links three of the Alto Genal's most attractive villages, leading you through some of the valley's most ancient chestnut groves.

A vaguely surreal experience awaits when you reach Júzcar, known locally as El Pueblo de los Pitufos or The Smurf Village. This former white village was painted blue in 2011 when the village was chosen as a centrepiece of the Sony film *The Smurfs in 3D*. So many visitors came – 80,000 in the first six months – that the local economy was transformed and the villagers have since voted to stick with their newfound blue-dom. Be prepared for three stiff climbs during the course of this beautiful circuit.

The walk begins in front of the town hall at the centre of Cartajima: you'll see signs for the *ayuntamiento* (town hall) as you enter the village. With your back to the town hall turn right, then right again down a flight of steps. After passing a ceramic sign describing mosto wine, turn right again passing in front of house number 15. At the end of the street turn once more right then reaching a fork take the lower, left option. The road's surface turns from concrete to dirt.

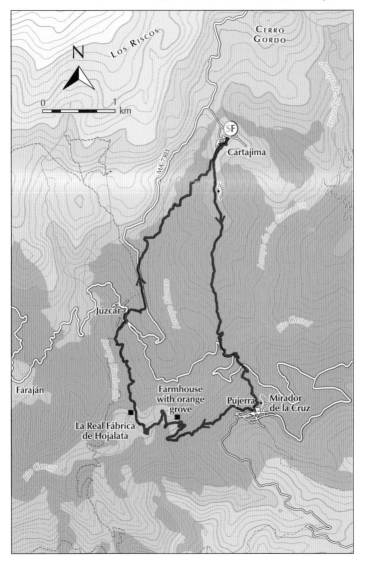

Reaching a fork by a pylon keep right. At the next fork take the left track which leads along a ridgetop, shortly passing a ramshackle breeze-block building. Leaving the track via a flight of steps to your left you reach a *mirador* (viewing point).

Exit the mirador's picnic area at its southern end to rejoin the track, which runs on along the ridgetop before beginning to descend as Pujerra comes into sight to the south. Some 100m after passing between a small group of cork oaks you reach a fork just beyond two square, metal drain covers. Keep left, immediately passing between two cork oaks then after just 5m, at the next fork, keep right and continue to loop down towards the valley floor.

After passing the entrance to Villa Ciri Lo the track reaches a road just to the right of a white hut. Cut left, cross a bridge over the **Río Genal**, then 50m beyond the river, just as the road swings hard to the right, angle left off the road along a track. After 15m cut right up a narrow footpath. Climbing steeply past a rocky outcrop the path braids then joins again after 20m. Reaching the road you left earlier head straight across and continue to climb steeply through the oaks and chestnuts.

Reaching a fork where up to the right you'll see a green marker post, keep left on the clearer track. Bearing right past a pylon the track climbs and after crossing a stream bed runs up to the **Mirador de la Cruz**. ◄ With your back to the mirador go right, past a signboard about the surrounding chestnut forest, El Castañar. The road climbs steeply past the first houses of **Pujerra**. Reaching a junction continue up Calle Arriero to reach the small square of Plaza Vieja and a statue of the Visgothic King Wamba (1hr 35min).

A signboard identifies the surrounding landmarks.

Legend tells that **Wamba**, a goatherd from Pujerra, was chosen to be King of the Visigoths. Reluctant to accept the title he declared himself to be but a simple peasant saying, 'Only when my staff grows leaves will I agree to be your king'. He then struck the ground with the staff which miraculously burst into leaf. Wamba then accepted that in spite of his reticence it was his destiny to become king.

Exit the square by bearing right past house number 14, then reaching a fork by house number 9 go right. Angling right and descending past house number 7 the road bears left to reach a fork. Take the lower, left-hand branch along a dirt track which descends through a group of ancient chestnuts as views open out towards Cartajima. After passing through a metal gate the track describes a sharp loop to the right as the smurf-blue houses of Júzcar come into sight. Reaching a fork go right, sticking to the most clearly defined track. At the next fork, looping right, you shortly pass through a second metal gate.

The track passes above a **farmhouse with an orange grove**, then passing a row of vines then angling right leads through a third metal gate before descending through a stand of ancient cork oaks. Approaching the river the track bears hard left where you pass through a fourth metal gate. Running parallel to the river the track

Chestnut grove with logs between Pujerra and Júzcar

eventually angles right then once more hard left before crossing a stream bed to reach a metal gate. Just before the gate cut right, down to the Genal.

Reaching the Genal go left along an indistinct path for some 50m then cross the river to pick up a narrow footpath that leads through a stand of *caña* (a bamboo-type plant). After angling left it becomes clearer as way-marking posts topped by blue arrows appear. The path adopts a course running up the right side of the gorge of the **Arroyo Riachuelo** whose waters once drove the bellows of **La Real Fábrica de Hojalata** (The Royal Tin Factory) which is just out of sight, down to your left.

LA REAL FÁBRICA DE HOJALATA DE JÚZCAR

Built on the orders of Philip V of Spain, hence the 'Royal' of its name, the factory produced tin between 1725 and 1788 at a time when the metal was used to protect the hulls of the Spanish fleet. The precariousness of the factory's water supply in times of drought, together with the increased cost of sourcing wood for its furnaces when local sources became depleted, led to its abandonment.

After passing into private hands the factory was bought in 2001 by an economist from Madrid who restored its buildings and planted an organic vineyard. His white moscatel wine was recently voted 'Best white wine of Andalucía'.

After passing through a gate made of an old bed base the path continues to climb as views open out to the south. Reaching a junction where to your right you'll see a galvanised metal gate, maintain your course, climbing over another gate made of a single bed base.

The blue houses of **Júzcar** come into view as the path widens to become a track that climbs steeply past a number of smallholdings. Reaching a fork, keep right. The track becomes concreted. At the next fork, maintain your course and climb past the first houses of Júzcar, among which number 17 remains defiantly white. Continuing up Calle Sol you reach a junction opposite Hotel Bandolero. Turn left (3hr 5min).

Reaching a metal bench cut right up Calle Solete. Climbing steeply past the last village houses and the village water deposit the track bears left before reaching the **MA-7303**. Turning left along the road for 500m you reach a sign for 'Cartajima 50min, PRA-224'.

Here go right, away from the road down through chestnut groves along a broad track. At the first fork keep right, sticking to the main track. ▶ Looping down towards the valley floor the track crosses a stream bed where the track's ancient cobbling is visible. After crossing the course of the **Arroyo Blanco** follow the track on up towards Cartajima. Reaching the junction you passed at the beginning of the walk, cut left then retrace your footsteps back to **Cartajima** (4hr).

Close encounter of the Smurf kind

Cartajima comes into sight along with the jagged southern face of Los Riscos.

WALK 11
Alpandeire circuit

Start/Finish	La Iglesia de San Antonio de Padua, Alpandeire
Distance	3.8km
Ascent/Descent	225m
Grade	Easy/Medium
Time	1hr 15min
Refreshments	None en route

This short down-then-up circuit describes a gentle loop through the beautiful valley that lies southwest of Alpandeire. The walk is just 3.8km in length, the shortest in this guide, but the steep climb back up to the village provides a good leg stretch, there are soaring views out to the south and west, and this could offer a memorable introduction to the chestnut-clad hillsides of the Genal valley.

The walk begins at the main entrance to the church of San Antonio at the centre of Alpandeire. With your back to the portal turn left, climb a flight of steps, then cut left. Reaching a fork go straight ahead, descending past Hotel Casa Grande. The road bears sharply right past a monument to Fray Leopoldo then descends to reach a white building with twin air conditioning units.

Fray Leopoldo de Alpandeire (1864–1956) was born in the village. He lived many years of his life in Granada where he became a Capuchin monk and was later known, and venerated, thanks to his charitable work with the poor of the city. He was beatified in 2010 when five members of a Vatican council declared that his curing of a sick man had been a miracle.

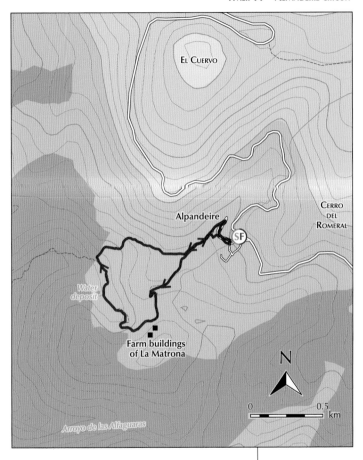

Here cut hard round left for 75m. Ignoring GR141 waymarking pointing right towards Ronda, maintain your course. Reaching a house with a horsewheel motif above its door, El Majano, keep right. ▶ The track reverts to dirt, leading on past a spring and a water trough, as you descend steeply into the valley. Looping hard left then right the track levels as it passes by a walnut grove then

Ahead of you the farm buildings of **La Matrona** are now visible, straddling the ridgetop that lies to the south.

The view west across the Genal valley towards Atajate

climbs for 100m to reach a fork. Cut right down a narrow, concrete track that leads down to the valley floor through stands of evergreens, cork oaks and chestnut.

After a leafy descent the track loops hard right past a spring, then angling left passes between two sets of green gates before running on past groves of citrus.

After passing to the right of a **water deposit** the track reaches a large black gate with stone pillars next to a drain cover. Here cut right up a narrow path, shortly passing a water deposit with a horse's head scratched into its render. Just before reaching a white building, where the hillside has been quarried to your right, you reach a fork where you should turn left.

Reaching a gate marked 'Por favor, no pasar. Finca Privada', cut right up a narrow path that climbs steeply between fences, cobbled in parts. At a point where the path becomes overgrown, go left then right, following a less distinct path along the edge of an abandoned olive grove where mistletoe has taken hold. At the top of the grove the path angles left across open ground. Cutting right it climbs past a large, solitary white gate post where

you pick up the clearer, cobbled footpath you left earlier. Winding its way on upwards, flanked in parts by agave, the path descends to reach the track you followed out of the village. Turn left.

Spring passed on the descent from the village

Reaching the house with the horse wheel motif, El Majano, turn right along Calle del Algarrobo. Some 25m past house number 65 cut sharp left and at the next junction turn right into Calle Pósito. Reaching a second junction go straight ahead. Cut left at a telephone box then climb a flight of steps to return to your point of departure (1hr 15min).

WALK 12

Estación de Benaoján to Estación de Jimera de Líbar

Start	Benaoján train station
Finish	Jimera de Líbar train station
Distance	8.5km
Ascent	45m
Descent	140m
Grade	Easy
Time	2hr
Refreshments	In Estación de Jimera
Transport	Trains depart from Jimera back to Benaoján at around 1.00pm, 5.00pm and 8.00pm (check at www.renfe.com). The journey takes just 7 minutes.

This short, easy walk follows a pretty riverside path that links the sleepy village of Benaoján with the sleepier-still hamlet of Jimera de Líbar, following the course of the Guadiaro river and that of the Ronda to Algeciras railway.

You could combine the walk with lunch at Restaurante Quercus (closed Mondays), or the colourful Bar Allioli (closed Tuesdays) before returning by train to your point of departure: train times dovetail nicely if you get going by around 11am. Alternatively, you could make an early start then take the late morning train back to Benaoján Estación.

Head south along the platform, drop down to the road and continue past Bar Stop. After 75m turn left and cross a level crossing. The road drops down, crosses the river Guadiaro and reaches a sign for 'Sendero Río Guadiaro, 7.3km'. Turn right along a track that hugs the left bank of the river. Soon you pass an **abandoned farm** with three dead palm trees.

The track crosses a small **wooden bridge** then bears right, narrows, and passes a ruined farm (20min). The path, rockier in sections and clearly marked with GR249

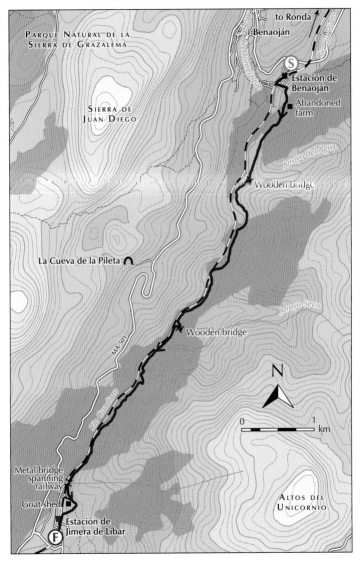

Looking west across the valley towards La Sierra de Benaoján

marker posts, runs close to the side of the Guadiaro, leading past a section of pole fencing at the bank's steepest point. Looping away from the river, it crosses a stream via another small **wooden bridge** before angling back towards the Guadiaro.

Soon a concrete water channel runs immediately to the left of the path and you pass a rusting black and white sign for Ojo al Tren (1hr 40min).

The **Bobadilla–Ronda–Algeciras railway line**, one of Europe's most spectacular stretches of track, was built between 1888 and 1892 by a British engineering company with funding from the financier Sir Alexander Henderson (Lord Faringdon). The company operated the line until 1913 when its operation was handed over to the Spanish State.

The journey by train from Ronda to Algeciras numbers among the most beautiful in Europe, taking you through the spectacular gorge at Colmenar: it recently featured in the BBC series *Great Continental Railway Journeys*.

In another 40m a **metal bridge** spans the railway: don't cross here but continue straight on, passing left of a **goat shed** along a narrow path which soon merges with a broad track. Passing a ramshackle fence made of railway sleepers, the track crosses a bridge before reaching a crossroad. Turn right.

Dropping down a concrete track past the first houses of Estación de Jimera de Líbar, you reach a junction next to the railway line. Turn left and follow the station fence, passing by Bar Allioli, to reach a tunnel that leads to the **train station** (2hr). ▶

Looking back to Benaoján

Trains back to Benaoján stop on the far side of the track; tickets can be bought at the station or on the train.

WALK 13

Estación de Benaoján to
La Cueva de la Pileta

Start/Finish	Estación de Benaoján
Distance	7.7km
Ascent/Descent	250m
Grade	Easy
Time	2hr 5min
Refreshments	None en route

This pretty there-and-back walk leads you from the sleepy Estación de Benaoján up to La Cueva de la Pileta, one of the most fascinating underground excursions in Europe. Most of the walk is by way of a broad farm track that leads through a beautiful expanse of *dehesa* (forest which has been partially cleared to leave selected species eg evergreen and cork oaks). You return by way of the same path. If you were to set off mid-morning you could visit the cave then have a leisurely picnic among the oak trees.

The walk begins beneath the platform clock at Estación de Benaoján. From here head south past Bar La Cantina. At the end of the platform continue along the road past Bar/Restaurante Stop. As you reach a level crossing turn right at a sign for La Tienda de Annie. Follow the road round to the left, cross a bridge over the Santo then reaching a junction turn right. Some 15m past the entrance to Molino del Santo turn left along a broad track following a sign, 'Sendero'.

After 100m you reach twin gate posts, one post marked 'Dehesa de Benaoján' and the other 'Camino Privado'. If the main gate is closed pass through a small wire-and-post gate to its right and continue along the track.

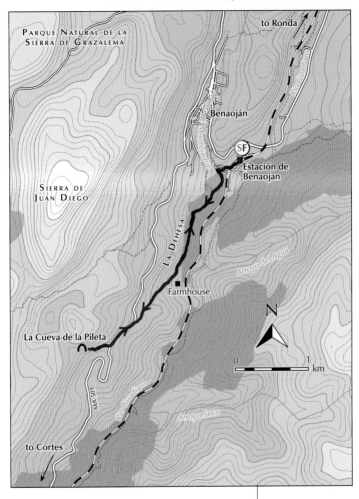

Reaching a fork keep right along the more clearly defined track which runs gently on through **La Dehesa de Benaoján**. After 200m ignore a sign pointing right for Camino del Chorrito and continue along the track

The ticket office at Benaoján station

through a swathe of dehesa for approx. 1.3km. Some 50m before reaching the gates to a **farmhouse**, the home of a sculptor – you'll see his creations in the garden ahead of you – go right, up a narrow path marked by a cairn (35min) which leads to a wire-and-post gate.

Beyond the gate, angling slightly left, the path crosses a stream bed then continues to climb, hugging its left bank. Where the stream bed ends bear slightly left and continue on up the most clearly defined path: cairns mark your way. Eventually, having crossed a second stream bed the path angles sharply right and leads up to another wire-and-post gate. Some 15m beyond the gate you reach a road, the **MA-501**, by twin blue and white chevrons.

Turn left and follow the road south for 450m. Reaching a sign for La Cueva de la Pileta and a signboard for Ruta de los Parques Naturales turn right and follow the road as it angles left to reach another signboard for La Cueva de la Pileta. Climb the flight of steps just left of the signboard and follow a narrow footpath with a metal handrail up to the entrance of **La Cueva de la Pileta** (1hr 10min). After visiting the cave retrace your footsteps back to **Estación de Benaoján** (2hr 5min).

LA CUEVA DE LA PILETA

The Pileta cave was discovered in 1905 by a farmer, José Bullón Lobato, who lived at the farm in the valley below. When searching for bat guano to fertilise his fields he lowered himself through a narrow opening in the rocks before discovering a series of caverns stretching deep into the mountainside. They contain some of the most remarkable cave paintings in Europe, spanning a period of some 25,000 years.

The existence of the cave was revealed to a wider audience by a British officer from Gibraltar who visited the cave while on an outing to find eagles' nests. It was subsequently visited and documented by the French archaeologist Henri Breuil who documented some 50 paintings within the cavern complex.

Ownership and management remains in the hands of the descendants of José Bullón Lobato in spite of attempts by the Spanish government to expropriate the cave.

Opening times vary according to the season and it's wise to pre-book rather than turn up on spec. See www.cuevadelapileta.org

WALK 14

Estación de Jimera circuit

Start/Finish	Plaza de San Roque, Estación de Jimera
Distance	11km
Ascent/Descent	150m
Grade	Medium
Time	3hr
Refreshments	Bars and shops in Jimera de Líbar
Access	Arriving at Estación de Jimera on the MA-8307 cut left down to the station then bear right past recycling bins to reach the Plaza de San Roque. If arriving by train pass through the pedestrian tunnel at the southern end of the platform then turn left to reach the start point of the walk.

This short walk describes a lazy loop in the Guadiaro river valley, taking you through two quiet villages, both with bars and restaurants. Early in the walk you follow an ancient, cobbled footpath from the railway line up to Jimera de Líbar before following broad farm tracks back down into the valley. In the warmer months you could swim in the river as you approach Estación de Jimera towards the end of the walk.

The walk begins in the Plaza de San Roque in Estación de Jimera on the east side of the Ronda–Algeciras railway line, in front of Bar Allioli. With your back to the bar turn right along the road which runs parallel to the railway. At the end of the street cut right at a sign, 'Sendero Río Guadiaro', along Calle Fuente Grande. The road climbs gently to reach a junction next to a black metal gate. Turn right following a sign, 'Camino Huertas Nuevas/Cuesta de la Barca'.

A concrete track leads past two houses, the second marked 'Alquería Veracruz'. Reaching a fork the main track angles right, climbs then cuts hard right. Continue straight ahead, leaving the track, to pick up a path that

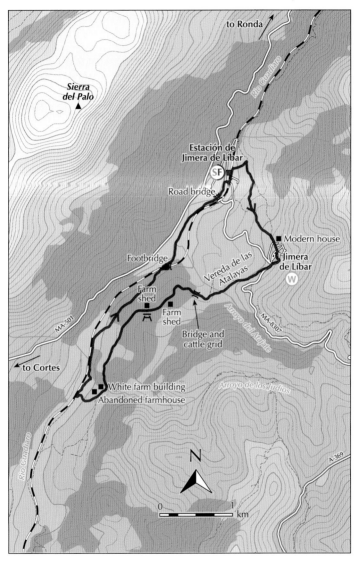

runs along the bottom of an olive grove. Climbing more steeply the path becomes cobbled in sections. Passing behind a water deposit the path runs on between olive groves, then bearing left passes just right of the entrance gates to a **modern house** where you reach a tarmac road.

Here turn right and follow Calle Prado into the centre of **Jimera de Líbar**, passing first a school, then Hotel Inz Almaraz, then the Unicaja bank. At the end of the street, bearing right, you reach the Plaza de Nuestra Señora Virgen de la Salud (30min).

Cross to the square's far side, pass just left of the church along Avenida Majestral Carillo then turn left down Calle Taramas. Bearing left you reach a junction. Turn right and continue down to a second junction opposite a children's play area.

Here turn left along the **MA-8307** for 75m, then just before reaching the km5 post bear right along a broad farm track following GR waymarking. Just beyond a farm with a netted perimeter fence go left at a sign, 'Vereda de

La Sierra Blanquilla on the Guadiaro's western side

las Atalayas' along a narrower dirt track to reach a fork just beneath the gates of a farm. ▸

Here take the lower, right-hand fork and descend along a broad path, the **Vereda de las Atalayas**. The path, cobbled in sections, runs down to the track that you left earlier. Bear left, cross a **bridge** then a **cattle grid** and continue along the broad farm track ignoring a footpath to the right marked 'Sendero'. Passing right of a **farm shed** the track enters an area of *dehesa* (forest which has been partially cleared to leave selected species) dotted with cork oak. Passing between a second **farm shed** and a **picnic area** the track runs on past a round corral and two more farm buildings before leading on through a green metal gate (1hr 15min).

Descending gently the track's surface becomes more rutted: it can be muddy here following rain. Eventually the track angles hard to the right and crosses the stream bed of the **Arroyo de los Judios** beyond which you pass above a **white farm building**. From here continue parallel to the fence for some 75m then go right, through a gap in the fence and follow a less distinct track which passes just above an **abandoned farmhouse**. After descending for 150m the track cuts right before descending to a wire-and-post gate (1hr 40min).

Beyond the gate turn right along a narrow footpath which crosses a stream bed, then runs on close to the **railway line**, which is to your left. After crossing a water pipe then passing through a green gate, you shortly cross the **Arroyo de los Judios** a second time. The footpath runs on close to a fence and the railway line. Crossing two more stream beds it crosses more open ground before passing through a gate made of a wooden pallet and bed base.

Angling slightly uphill and away from the railway the path cuts through thick clumps of cistus as Jimera de Líbar comes into sight. Eventually, after crossing another stream bed, the path runs up to a sign for Via Pecuaria. Just beyond the sign, passing through a wire-and-post gate, you reach the railway line. Go right, cross the track via a newly built **footbridge** (or cross directly across the

At this point there are fine views out west to the jagged peaks of La Sierra Blanquilla.

Looking north along the valley towards the train station

tracks, avoiding the bridge) then continue northwards along a leafy lane which runs between the railway track and the **Río Guadiaro**.

Passing three millhouses – there's a lovely bathing spot beside the second mill – the track runs between walnut groves, passes left of a road bridge then reaches a roundabout. Head straight on, passing beneath a second road **bridge**.

Continue parallel to the river until you reach a sign pointing back the way you've just come, Cañada Real del Campo de Gibraltar. Turn right then pass beneath the railway via a tunnel for pedestrians. Reaching the road by recycling bins turn left to return to your point of departure, La Plaza de San Roque (3hr).

WALK 15

Cortes de la Frontera
circuit via Los Pinos

Start/Finish	Mesón Los Alcornocales, Cortes de la Frontera
Distance	13km; if not climbing Los Pinos: 10.5km
Ascent/Descent	875m; if not climbing Los Pinos: 700m
Grade	Difficult; if not climbing Los Pinos: Medium/Difficult
Time	5hr; if not climbing Los Pinos: 3hr 40min
Refreshments	None en route
Access	From Ronda take the A-374 towards Sevilla. After approx 2km go left on the MA-7401 towards Montejaque. Just past Benaoján go left on the MA-8401 to Cortes de la Frontera. Mesón Los Alcornocales is on the right as you enter the village.

This challenging circuit leads through wild and rocky terrain to the summit of Los Pinos (1395m), one of the Sierra de Grazalema's highest peaks and most stunning viewing points. If an 875m climb is a little too much for you, this can be reduced by some 250m by cutting out the final ascent to the summit from Los Llanos del Puerto: you'll still have the most memorable of hikes. Expect extraordinary karst limestone formations, ancient cobbled footpaths, soaring views, ancient stands of oaks and few other walkers on this magnificent full-day walk.

The walk begins at Mesón Los Alcornocales on the north-east side of Cortes de la Frontera. From here head towards the village centre then passing a bus stop cut up to the right, then left, then once more right past a children's play area to reach a marker post 'PRA252 Montejaque' and a narrow footpath. Turn right. The path passes above blocks of flats then winds left past a small stone hut to reach a track. Head straight on to pick up the continuation of the path which climbs steeply up past a *calera* (limekiln) to meet with the track you crossed earlier.

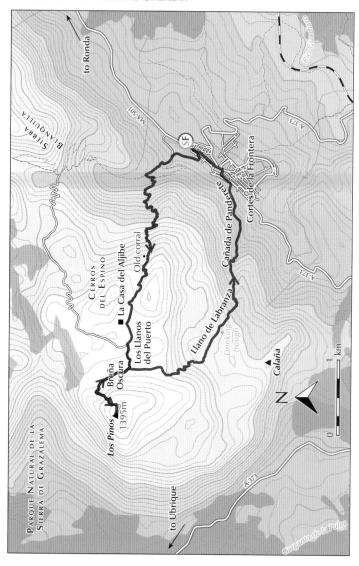

Turn left along the track then after 125m, just beyond a drainage channel, cut right at a marker post on a footpath that angles right then leads through a wire-and-post gate. The path, cobbled in places, loops steeply upwards through the gorse and evergreen oaks as Jimera de Líbar comes into view to the northeast, beyond the Guadiaro valley. After a steep climb the trees begin to thin out as the path becomes sandier, before angling left it runs towards a fence. Follow the path as it loops sharply right, adopting a straighter course where drystone walling supports its lower right-hand edge.

Looking north on the ascent from Cortes towards La Sierra Blanquilla

You'll now see the fence above you to your left. After approximately 175m cut left, away from the path, along a less distinct path which leads up through a gap in the rusting metal fence where the wire-and-post gate is often left open.

The footpath loops up and up, through a stand of evergreen oaks then leads through a double gate of galvanised metal.

Beyond the gate the path loops on up through the oaks and boulders. Passing by the remains of an **old corral** the path loops hard left then once more right. You shortly cross a flatter area where a line of stones on the ground marks the path which passes just left of a fenced enclosure with a faded sign marked 'bebedero'. After reaching the top of the pass the path cuts through rocky ground where reafforestation is taking place, the young saplings having been netted against grazing goats. Here you reach a second depression in the rock.

Here cut sharply left past more netted saplings: after some 30m the path becomes much clearer as it loops up to the top of the next pass. Descending, and following cairns down into another depression the path cuts across its flat, grassy base where, passing just right of low-growing hawthorns, it then angles left then right to cross a low rise.

Skirting round to the left of another depression among rocks, you descend to reach a red and white GR marker post. Bearing right, you soon come to two more marker posts. Cut right between the posts to reach the abandoned mountain refuge of **La Casa del Aljibe** (2hr 10min). ◄ The roof of the building channelled rainwater down into a subterranean water tank, thus the house's name ('House of the water tank').

This is a fine spot to break for a picnic.

Returning to the point where you left the path to reach La Casa del Aljibe, continue along a wide, grassy track for 300m to reach a junction and another marker post. Taking the left fork, descend to reach a flat area among the rocks, **Los Llanos del Puerto** (2hr 15min). ◄

If you don't intend to climb Los Pinos you can cut left here and reduce the walk's length by 1hr 20min.

If climbing to the summit cut right across Los Llanos del Puerto. Reaching a marker post you pick up a narrow footpath which, after passing a small fenced enclosure, cuts left through a gap in a fence. The path now climbs up the east flank of the mountainside, marked by cairns, through an expanse of oaks known locally as **Breña Oscura**. Eventually, passing left of a small enclosure protecting two fir trees, one living, the other dead, climb straight ahead to reach the trig point at the summit of **Los Pinos** (1395m) (3hr).

The trig point atop El Cerro de Los Pinos, 1395m

From the summit of **Los Pinos** a stunning 360 degree panorama encompasses the mountains of the southern ranges of Los Alcornocales, the summits of La Concha and Los Reales, the rolling farmlands stretching west towards Jerez and Sevilla along with the Sierra de Algodonales, the peaks of Lagarín and La Graja above El Gastor, the Sierra de Ronda and the Sierra de Antequera. And on clear days Gibraltar, the mountains of North Africa as well as the distant Sierra Nevada are also visible.

From the peak make your way back down to Los Llanos del Puerto (3hr 35min). Bear right and continue east along a broad, level track. At the point where the track ends at a marker post, where a fence runs to your right, head slightly left to pick up a path which zigzags down towards the **Llano de Labranza**.

Shortly before reaching the valley floor the path angles right and runs on through the rock before it descends to reach the valley floor and a marker post.

Continue straight ahead through the rocks, passing a faded red and white paint flash on a boulder. With a rocky outcrop just to your right you pass just left of a stone corral built up against the rocks, then a low **drinking trough** hewn from a solid rock.

From here continue along a straight section of path marked with stones to either side which soon begins to thread its way down through a thick stand of broom. Angling slightly right the path passes by a tumbledown hunters' shelter, then angling right round an outcrop of rock runs towards the end of a ridge. Head steeply down to the left, looking for cairns, on a path which loops down towards the head of the **Cañada del Panderete** gorge. After a steep descent the path cuts back and forth between the valley's northern and southern flanks, overgrown in parts.

Eventually the path angles away from the valley floor, now lined with agaves and supported by a stone wall to its right. Cutting between groves of olives the path merges with a concrete track which descends towards the village, passing pens where hunting dogs are kept. Reaching a junction go left, then arriving at a tarmac road head straight across and drop down Calle Alta. Take the next street to the right, next to a traffic mirror.

Reaching the main road through the village turn left, pass the bullring then reaching a fork maintain your course. Passing a supermarket you return to your point of departure, **Mesón Los Alcornocales** (5hr).

WALK 16

Cortes de la Frontera southern circuit

Start/Finish	Bar La Cafetería, Cortes de la Frontera (next to the bullring)
Distance	12.7km
Ascent/Descent	475m
Grade	Medium
Time	3hr 15min
Refreshments	Bars and shops in Estación de Cortes at 35mins

Although this is a medium grade, three to four hour walk, you could easily take far longer if you explore along the way. The Casa de la Piedra makes a fascinating diversion, numbering among the Guadiaro valley's most unusual archaeological sites. After descending to the valley floor from Cortes, then traversing the railside settlement of Estación de Cortes, you climb steeply to La Torre del Paso which stands on a high bluff overlooking the Guadiaro valley. This is an enchanting spot for a lazy picnic-with-a-view. Be ready for a steep final pull at the end of the walk back up to Cortes where there are several lively bars to slake your thirst.

The walk begins in front of a map of local footpaths next to Bar La Cafetería on the northern side of Cortes de la Frontera. With your back to the map turn left, then reaching a post box take the first left down Paseo de Las Acacias. Reaching a junction in front of the village **cemetery** turn right to reach a fork where you should take the lower, left-hand option passing a No Entry sign. At the end of this street turn left. After passing a motorcycle shop go left at a marker post down a rough track. Passing beneath two unfinished apartment blocks you reach a junction by a spring where waymarking points left, downhill. Ignore this path but stick to the wider track, maintaining your course.

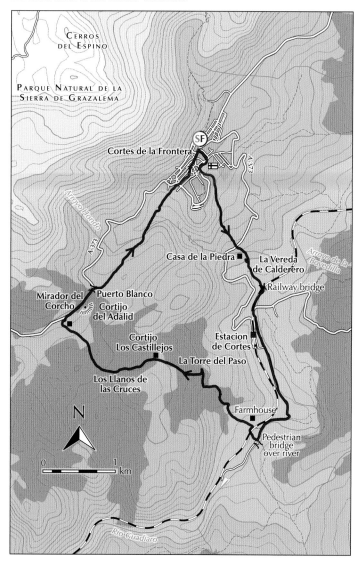

The track gradually angles round to the east, then becoming concreted drops down to reach the **A-373**. Head straight across and continue to descend a narrower footpath, **La Vereda de Calderero**, which after 30m crosses the **Arroyo Hondo** via a small stone bridge. Continuing your descent along the old, cobbled path you reach a damaged signboard. Cut left through a wire-and-post gate to visit the **Casa de la Piedra**.

Theories vary as to the origin of the **Casa de la Piedra** whose inner chamber and exterior decoration have been hollowed out of a single sandstone boulder. According to some sources it began life as a Visigothic place of worship while others claim that it was a clandestine Mozarabic chapel built by Christians for worship during the Moorish period. What is certain is that it was later used as a wine press. Part of the original press can still be seen as well as the vats which were used to store the wine.

The Casa de la Piedra's ornate sandstone carving

After dropping down past a small farm that spans both sides of the path it widens to become a track that leads beneath a **railway bridge**. Immediately beyond the bridge cut right. Reaching the A-373 once again, continue on your same course then, reaching a 50kmph sign, go left following a sign for El Gecko and follow the road for some 1.5km through the linear, railside settlement of **Estación de Cortes**. Leaving the last houses of the village behind, the track runs up to a junction where to your left a **pedestrian bridge** spans the river (1hr 5min).

Here cut right up a broad track which leads across the railway line then angles right and passes behind a house. After a few yards cut left through a gate made of old bed bases then follow the old *cañada* (public footpath or drovers' path) between stone walls up past a **farmhouse**.

Shortly the footpath becomes overgrown but by cutting left then right, continue on upwards, parallel to the old footpath which now runs just to your left. Passing a tumbledown wall maintain your course to the top of the next field where, bearing right, you pick up the footpath once again: it has been deeply rutted by cattle and is overgrown in parts but is easy enough to follow, still climbing steeply through a stand of oaks.

Reaching another more open area the path passes just to the right of a rocky outcrop, running parallel to a wall to your right. After passing beneath power lines you reach a wire-and-post gate, waymarked with white and blue stripes. Beyond the gate continue straight ahead then after 30m go left and continue your ascent, parallel to a drystone wall.

After passing through another gate marked 'Por favor Cierre' maintain your course to reach **La Torre del Paso** (1hr 40min).

> **La Torre del Paso** (watch tower), which has been recently restored, was built in the 13th century during the Moorish period. From its commanding position on a high bluff the trading route that ran along the Guadiaro valley could easily be vigilated.

Cortijo Los Castillejos

After visiting the tower return to the gate then cut right and climb between two stone walls. Shortly to your right you will spot a large threshing circle before you pass through a metal gate with GR waymarking. Beyond the gate continue straight ahead along a track which crosses a low rise. ▶ The track you've been following soon merges with the one leading to the farmhouse.

The buttressed farm building of Cortijo Los Castillejos comes into view to your right.

Maintain your course, ignoring tracks that lead to the left or right, as you traverse a flatter area, **Los Llanos de las Cruces**. Eventually the track loops right, crosses a cattle grid, then passes behind the farm buildings of **Cortijo del Adalid** (where the main house is signed 'Villa Marta') to reach the **A-373** (2hr 25min).

Turning right along the road you pass by the picnic area of **Mirador del Corcho**. From here you can follow a narrow footpath which runs just beneath the road which it joins after some 200m. Reaching **Puerto Blanco** the A-373 angles hard left. Cut right down a broad track. Passing a farm building the track narrows before it loops down to the valley floor, cobbled in sections. Crossing

Cows grazing in the evening light

the stream bed go right for 30m then cut left up a steep, eroded footpath.

Passing through a wire-and-post gate the path leads past a ramshackle farm to the southern side of the village where you reach a track. Go left to reach the first houses of Cortes and a junction. Head straight on to the far end of Calle Alcantarilla. Reaching houses numbered 1 and 2 cut left then right. After passing a tobacconist cut left again to reach the Plaza Carlos III and Cortes' elegant town hall. Climb the steps on the far side of the square then turn right along Calle Real. After passing a bank and a church you return to your point of departure (3hr 15min).

WALK 17
Benarrabá circuit via
Genalguacíl

Start/Finish	Hotel Banu Rabbah, Benarrabá (next to the village pool)
Distance	13km; shorter route avoiding Genalguacíl: 5.2km
Ascent/Descent	890m; shorter route avoiding Genalguacíl: 320m
Grade	Medium/Difficult; shorter route avoiding Genalguacíl: Medium
Time	4hr 10min; shorter route avoiding Genalguacíl: 1hr 30min
Refreshments	Bars and shops in Genalguacíl at 2hr

This figure-of-eight route makes for a moderately challenging day walk and links two beautiful, little-known villages. A good deal of the walk takes you along narrow paths where there are wonderful views out across the Genal valley and south towards the Mediterranean.

The route entails three sections of steep climbing, but the path is easy to follow and there are shady sections beneath the oak and chestnut trees which make the going easier in hot weather. It's possible to shorten the walk considerably by swinging right before crossing the Genal for the first time, but this would mean missing Genalguacíl, an exceptionally pretty village and a highlight of the walk.

From the hotel walk back towards the village, passing the football pitch then the school. Just past the school bear right, down Avenida Miguel Pérez Delgado, following a sign for Iglesia. Take the next right into Calle Sol. The street cuts sharply left then right. Reaching house number 16, cut right at a sign for 'La Portá, SLA175' on a dirt track that drops downhill away from the village.

As you loop downwards you'll see PR waymarking and white arrows. Reaching a solitary portal with a rickety crossbeam that serves no obvious purpose, the track loops left then right and resumes its course. It then loops

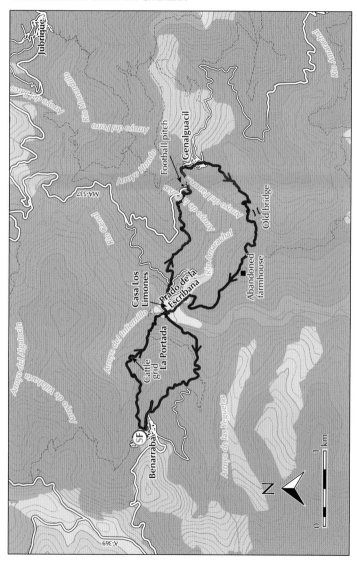

down past a citrus grove before cutting through a stand of ancient cork oaks.

The track contours gradually round the mountain and crosses a **cattle grid**. Beyond the grid the track runs uphill, levels and then descends for approximately 200m to a marker post for Genalguacíl. Cut left here and drop down on a steep, eroded path, which merges with a slightly wider path, marked by PR posts. The path narrows again, still loose and eroded in parts, before dropping down to meet a track beside the **Arroyo del Infiernillo**. Bearing right, you reach a low concrete **bridge** spanning the Río Genal (30min). ▸

Cross the river then turn left at a sign for 'Genalguacíl 2.3km' along the pebbly right bank of the Genal. After 125m cut right, away from the river, at a second sign for Genalguacíl, and follow a path that climbs steeply up behind the farm of **Casa Los Limones** (55min).

After climbing you pass through a small wooden gate then reach a track; here cross directly over the track and continue up through the cork oaks. Soon the path crosses

The path threading its way through the cork oaks

To cut the walk short, cut right just before the bridge along a broad track. Follow this, then turn right off the track after a line of pylons signed for Benarrabá.

133

the track once more and views open out across the Genal valley. The path runs up to meet the track for a third time (1hr 25min).

Go right and cross the track a final time. After 25m, just before reaching a gate, bear right at a marker post then continue along the footpath. It descends slightly, levels, then merges with a track which passes a pylon as it arcs round a gully before reaching a small farm. Turn left by a pylon and follow the path steeply upwards.

The path again merges with a track, which soon angles hard left and passes above a five-a-side **football pitch** before reaching a junction at the outskirts of **Genalguacíl**.

The village **names** of both Benarrabá and Genalguacíl, like most of those in this part of southern Spain, are of Berber origin: Benarrabá, from Banu Rabbah, translates as Sons of Rabbah while Genalguacíl – a corruption of Genna Alwacir – means Gardens of the Vizir.

Turn right and follow the tarmac road into the village centre, passing a tiled plaque and map showing the footpaths in the area south of Ronda. At the next fork keep right, passing the Fuente de la Alberquilla, then head all the way along Calle Real, past the Unicaja bank then the Casa Consistorial, to the church (2hr). Turning right you arrive at the village's beautiful main square, La Plaza de la Constitución.

Genalguacíl is unique in having an extraordinary collection of **street art** since inaugurating its biannual Encuentros de Arte when artists from throughout Spain are hosted by the village on the condition that they leave at least one piece of their work to the village.

Leave the square via the street running to the left of the church – the same one by which you entered. At the far end, just to the left of a *mirador* (viewpoint) with two contemporary sculptures, drop down a concrete road, and after just 40m swing sharp right along another concrete section of road.

Passing a line of wafer-bricked posts with wooden rails, the road divides. Fork left and drop steeply downhill, always sticking to the main path. You eventually come to a farm just to the right of the path, where there's a watering hole immediately in front of you. Go left and after just a few metres the path merges with a track which you follow downhill. The track soon reaches a junction with another track. Turn right and continue down to the bed of the Río Almarchal. Turn left on a track that cuts along the river's pebbly bank then runs up to a farm. In front of the farm cut right and cross the **Rio Almarchal**. ▶

Once you're over the river (2hr 35min), go left. Some 30m before reaching the ruined arch of an **old bridge** swing right, through the thick riverine vegetation on a narrow path that zigzags steeply up and away from the river. After passing beneath a salmon-coloured building the path climbs up to a track, where you bear left. The track loops left then right and continues climbing gradually upwards before levelling as it runs back towards the Genal.

You arrive at an **abandoned farmhouse** where the track divides. Fork right here. Soon you pass another ruin, then a modern house with a wooden cabin, before the track loops steeply back down towards the Almarchal river. Just before it reaches the river you meet with another track. Turn left and cross over the riverbed (3hr 10min).

The track cuts through a wooden fence then angles left to reach the flat meadow of **Prado de la Escribana**. Passing a children's climbing frame, you reach the **bridge** you crossed earlier in the walk. Cross back over the Genal and turn left along a broad track.

The track at first runs close to the Genal's right bank before it angles away from the river, now climbing steeply. Cross a cattle grid and after just 50m pass by a spring (which can be dry at the end of the summer months). Carry on up the main track, which is concrete in

In the wetter months you may need to remove your boots to cross the river.

Arriving in Bennarabá

its steeper sections. Some 10m beyond the point where a line of pylons runs up to meet with your track (3hr 40min) turn right off the track at a sign for Benarrabá. Passing between two drain covers cut slightly left and climb steeply up to the village. The path eventually meets with the road by the school you passed earlier in the walk..

Turn right to arrive back at Hotel Banu Rabbah in **Benarrabá** (4hr 10min).

WALK 18

Gaucín circuit

Start/Finish	Repsol petrol station in Gaucín (beside the A-369)
Distance	11.8km
Ascent/Descent	630m
Grade	Medium
Time	2hr 50min
Refreshments	None en route

This route makes for a rewarding half-day walk out from Gaucín. It is clearly waymarked, and there are fine views westwards across the Guadalete valley, while the ancient stands of cork oaks through which you pass are home to abundant birdlife.

There's a steep climb early in the walk as you head up the northeastern flank of El Hacho, and another at the end of the walk when you head back up to Gaucín. After following a narrow, rocky path early in the day there's a longish section of forestry track mid-walk, where you can abandon yourself to the views of the Sierra del Pino and the Sierra del Líbar.

You may meet with teams of corkcutters if you're undertaking the walk in the winter months: the oaks are particularly memorable when seen after their cork has been recently removed.

From the petrol station in Gaucín head north along Calle Camino del Montoro. At house number 16 cut left and pick up a path that runs just to the left of a line of eucalyptus trees. The path climbs steeply up between two fences, past groves of olives and almonds. Blue waymarking marks the way at this point.

▶ When you reach a fork keep left and continue to climb. Shortly, the path swings hard to the right and runs on, now parallel to a track just above you, before passing just the left fork and continue climbing to a pylon at the top of the ridge (25min).

Ahead you'll be able to spot the path you'll soon be following, cutting across the northern flank of El Hacho.

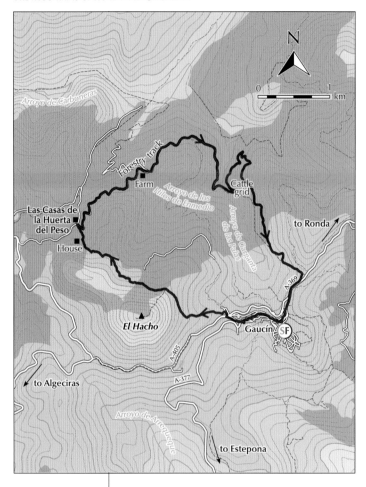

Here, passing a fallen wire-and-post gate, go left along a narrow path that winds through the rocks and the dense undergrowth beneath the oaks and conifers, with small ceramic plaques marking the way. Reaching a fence, you pass through a new wire-and-post gate.

Looking back to Gaucín as you leave the village

Beyond the gate the path angles right and descends towards a pylon; a few metres before reaching the pylon cut left and continue along the narrow path that runs past an old limekiln before descending to another gate with GR waymarking.

Beyond the gate go left along a wider path. When you reach a rocky defile to the left of the path, bear left and follow the path through the breach in the hillside. Here the path angles left, crosses a stream, then loops right. At an indistinct fork cut right, following blue waymarking, and pass through a new wooden-posted gate. At another fork 25m beyond the gate turn right.

After descending, then heading left and crossing a stream, the path reaches a fence and another wooden-posted gate. Beyond the gate, descending a flight of concrete steps you reach a track leading to a **house**, which is visible just to your left. Bearing right down the track, towards a pylon, you reach a junction with a broader track (1hr 5min).

Turn right, ignoring GR 'wrong way' waymarking, along a broad forestry track that passes above the

Breach in the mountainside at the top of the pass above Gaucín

buildings of **Las Casas de la Huerta del Peso**. The track gradually descends as views open out to the west. Passing an area where the hillside has been quarried, then a **farm** where pigs and goats are raised, you reach a junction. Carry straight on, ignoring a left fork downwards marked 'Finca La Capellania'.

Continue along the main track, which contours lazily around the valley. After looping sharply left and crossing the stream of **Los Hilos de Enmedio**, in a few hundred metres the track crosses a second stream, the **Arroyo de Garganta de las Palas**. Here the track loops left, crosses a **cattle grid**, then runs on for about 600m and crosses a third stream bed where huge rocks shore up the hillside.

Some 225m beyond the stream look for a sign for Camino de Gaucín a Cortes in a tree to the right of the track, and a ceramic plaque marked 'V' (1hr 50min). Bear sharply right, away from the track, and follow a path up through the heather, gorse, lavender and cork oaks.

The vast stands of **cork oak** (*Quercus suber*) are a defining feature of this region, hence the name of El

Leafy footpath leading back up to Gaucín

Parque Natural de los Alcornocales (cork oak park). The cork is harvested once every 10 to 12 years – the length of time it takes for the layer of bark, or cambium, to regenerate. Cork production is a major part of the local economy.

The path eventually passes through a gate made from an old bed base, where it broadens before merging with a broader track by a green metal gate. After passing a number of smallholdings the track leads up to the **A-369**. Turn right, then just beyond the municipal bandstand, reaching a stop sign, go left along Calle Queipo de Llano, parallel to a black metal railing.

After passing a roundabout head straight on along Calle Los Bancos, then arc right into Calle del Corral. Continue past the Unicaja bank and then, reaching a junction, continue straight ahead, passing right of Modas Teresa, to the end of Calle Barrio Alto. Bear right, and having passed the Guardía Civil (police) headquarters reach the **A-377** and your point of departure (2hr 50min).

WALK 19
Montejaque circuit

Start/Finish	Town hall, Montejaque
Distance	16.3km; via wet weather alternative: 17.2km
Ascent/Descent	710m; via wet weather alternative: 650m
Grade	Medium/Difficult
Time	4hr 55min; via wet weather alternative: 5hr 5min
Refreshments	None en route

This superb full-day walk leads you to the heart of the Grazalema Park and to an area of stunning natural beauty. Leaving Montejaque, you are first faced with a long climb to the top of the rocky Líbar valley. The terrain levels as you cross a series of broad, flat-bottomed valleys or *navas* before cutting down through some of the most beautiful karst limestone formations in the park. A mixture of tracks and narrow footpaths bring you back through oak forest and olive groves to Montejaque.

In case of wet weather an alternative ending is suggested, avoiding olive groves that can become difficult to negotiate after prolonged spells of rain.

Allow a full day to get the most out of this stunning itinerary. You should expect to pass close to cattle, but rest assured they are not *ganado bravo* (fighting bulls).

From in front of the Montejaque *ayuntamiento* (town hall), cut left along the side of a church beneath a row of palm trees and turn right into Calle Nueva. Passing a ceramic plaque and a cross, bear right into Calle Santa Cruz and then take the first street to the left, opposite El Hogar del Jubilado, and follow this street up through the village. Leaving the last houses behind you, pass several dog kennels built among the rock before meeting with a track at a GR marker post and a sign depicting birds found in the park (15min). Follow the track up the valley between the **Sierra de Juan Diego** and the **Sierra de Montalete**.

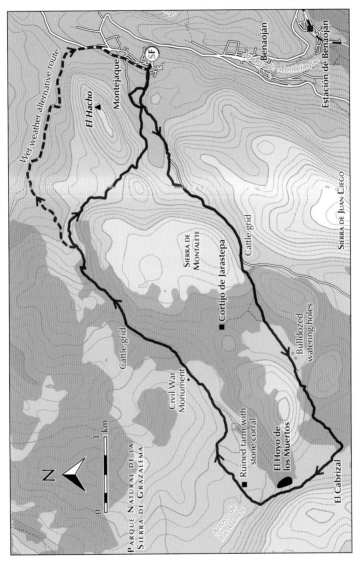

Grazing cattle at the edge of the first nava

Nearing the top of the pass you cross a **cattle grid**. In another 300m bear right off the track along a stony path leading to a green gate (55min), beyond which continue climbing up a cobbled path.

After passing to the right of a stone ruin, then crossing a dirt track, go through a black metal gate (it is sometimes left open). The path leads beneath a clump of oaks then crosses more open ground before meeting with a track. Turn right. The track soon begins to descend and you reach a red sign on an oak. Cut left off the track along a stony footpath. After 75m the path arcs left where cairns and paint flashes guide you through a stand of low oaks.

After angling right and descending, the path passes through a gap in a stone wall where it merges with a track which you follow across a vast field or nava. Having passed two **bulldozed watering holes** the track reaches a stone wall. Bear right, and then just beyond a large oak pass through a metal gate (1hr 25min).

Go left along a narrow path that runs just left of a stone wall. The path climbs, bears left and reaches a flatter

Centenarian oak trees at El Cabrizal

area. Angle sharply right, looking for cairns, on a narrow path that threads between the rocks and descends. After passing just left of a ruined hut the path leads through a gate made of metal mesh. Following cairns and making sure not to gain height, you reach another vast nava: **El Cabrizal** (1hr 55min).

Go right and cross the field; a huge stone arrow on the ground gives you your bearing, NNW. Crossing the field, you pass just left of a group of four huge oaks whose trunks meet at the base. At the far side of the field look for cairns and a second stone arrow, where you leave the field via an initially indistinct path which climbs up across the rocks and then becomes more clearly defined. Continue to a hollow with a stone-walled corral built against a cliff (2hr 25min). Keep left and stay high as you contour round this rocky depression, known to locals as **El Hoyo de los Muertos** (Dead Men's Hollow). The path leads over a low ridge to a wire-and-post gate.

Beyond the gate angle down across the hillside to a low stone wall and fence. Following these to the left,

145

you reach a wire-and-post gate topped by barbed wire. Beyond the gate cross the (dry) stream bed of the **Arroyo de los Álamos** then continue straight over a low ridge (there's no path), beyond which you descend to a vehicle track. Angle right and after a few metres, reaching a fork, take the left branch (2hr 50min).

You'll shortly see a **ruined farm with stone corrals** over to your right. Continue along the track, which leads on through a gate in a wall marked 'Cerrar la Puerta por favor' (Please Close the Gate). The track arcs left to reach a chain slung between metal posts. Some 20m beyond the chain cut right at a sign for Montejaque.

The path leads into a more wooded area where, after crossing a stream, it cuts up an eroded bank to reach a gate. Beyond the gate the path climbs, angles right, crosses a stream then runs up to a low stone wall. Go left and follow an indistinct vehicle track to the far end of the field where, passing through a metal gate, you reach another huge enclosure (3hr 20min).

Here leave the track (which arcs uphill) by cutting along the left bank of a stream. Soon you'll see a wall to your right. Sticking close to the wall you reach the far end of the enclosure where, after passing by a gate marked 'Propiedad Privada, Prohibido El Paso' (private property), you exit the enclosure via a small metal gate. Here the path merges with a track.

Descending steeply, pass a **monument** to the left of the track.

The **monument** marks the place where a landowner from Villaluenga (the 'D' of the inscription signifies Don or Sir) was assassinated in 1936, shortly after the outbreak of the Civil War. This part of Andalucía was the first part of Spain to fall to the Nationalist insurgents.

After a further 250m the track bears right and climbs. Having passed a **cattle grid** the track reaches the top of the rise where it merges with another track. Here go right and descend.

Rainbow on the descent towards Montejaque

Soon the track loops hard right then back left before dropping down to a junction where a smaller track angles up to the right.

Wet weather alternative finish
To avoid an olive grove that can be heavy going after prolonged rainfall, continue down the track (in other words don't branch right) to the bottom of the valley. Turn right and follow a broader track along the side of the dry reservoir of Montejaque to the MA-505. Turn right, and when you reach a water trough go right.

Head all the way along to the end of this street, then cut left then right to return to the square in **Montejaque**.

In dry weather, turn right at the junction. After climbing for 150m, just as the track loops hard right, cut left and follow an indistinct path marked by cairns down to a black metal gate (4hr). Beyond the gate the path, slightly overgrown in parts, runs between olive groves. At one point, running slightly uphill, the path becomes less distinct. Follow cairns on through the olives, being sure not to lose height. After 350m, heading down a steep bank to your left, you rejoin the path which loops left as it crosses a stream and then runs just to the right of a line of olives and oaks, marked by cairns. Crossing a low ridge just to the right of a rusting metal *coto* (hunting reserve) sign and cairn, the path levels then merges with a track that leads you through a wire-and-post gate (4hr 25min).

Beyond the gate the track levels before looping down into the valley you walked through at the beginning of the day. Reaching the valley floor, you pass by a stone hut topped by a weather vane and then come to a junction. Cut left along a newly surfaced concrete track. Passing the second of the village's water deposits cut right, down a narrow path between stone walls. After crossing a concrete water channel you reach the road by which you left the village earlier in the walk. Cut left here and retrace your footsteps back to the square in **Montejaque** (4hr 55min).

MONTEJAQUE

Montejaque's name is derived from Monte Xaquez meaning sacred or hidden mountain. A large fortress once stood on the site of the present village which was a vital link in Nasrid Granada's western line of defence. During the War of Independence the village gained fame when José de Águilar, a Montejaqueño, rallied a small force of 250 men to defeat a French army of 600 foot soldiers and 90 cavalry.

The limestone peaks surrounding the village are home to some of the most extensive cave systems in Iberia and the village has a small museum dedicated to *espeleología* or caving. The tortured nature of the terrain in this part of the Sierra meant that some of Andalucía's most infamous bandoleros chose the mountains close to the village as their refuge as did a number of Republicans during and after the Spanish Civil War.

THE SIERRA DE GRAZALEMA

Zahara de la Sierra and its Moorish castle (Walk 31)

149

Zahara and its reservoir seen during the dry Andalucían summer (Walk 24)

The Parque Natural de la Sierra de Grazalema lies just to the west of Ronda and straddles the provinces of Cádiz and Málaga. The park encompasses part of the most southwesterly mountain range in Europe, the tail-end of the Cordillera Bética. This rugged massif, predominantly composed of limestone and dolomite, rises steeply up from the rolling farmlands around Jerez to a height of nearly 1700m. Although the park is comparatively small compared to others in Andalucía – it covers an area of just 500 square kilometres – the terrain is extraordinarily varied. Jagged formations of karst limestone give way to poplar-lined valleys, thick stands of cork and evergreen oaks alternate with old groves of olives and almonds and with fields of wheat and barley.

The park was recently declared a UNESCO biosphere reserve thanks in part to the diversity of its plants and wildlife which is the result of unusual climatic conditions. Continental, Mediterranean and Atlantic influences are all present in the park and the exceptionally high level of precipitation means that the area is remarkably green by Andalucían standards.

Three walks are included in this section that lie just beyond the park boundaries: two begin in El Gastor and the other, the Canalizo circuit, begins close to Algodonales. All have a natural affinity with the other walks within the park and afford fine views south towards the Sierra del Pinar.

PLANTS AND WILDLIFE

The unusually wet winters explain the existence of the large stand of pinsapos or Spanish firs (*Abies pinsapo*) on the northern slopes of the Sierra del Pinar (Walk 23 leads you through the forest). Within the park is one of the most extensive stands of cork oak forest in Europe, with groves of olives and almonds as well as evergreen and deciduous oaks, carob and wild olives.

The variety of wildflowers is extraordinary: a third of all the species that grow in Iberia are to be found within the park. Spring is the most spectacular time of year – in late April and early May the flowers are at their best – but you can see interesting botanical species throughout the year. If you'd like a list of the more common species visit www.cicerone. co.uk/803/resources

The park is an ornithological wonderland with one of the major migratory routes between Europe and Africa running along the western fringe of the park. Several species of raptors are resident: booted, short-toed, Bonelli's and golden eagles can be easily spotted while it's not unusual to see a hundred or more griffon vultures (*Gyps fulvus*) on the wing. The largest colony in Europe inhabits the rocky ledges of the Garganta Verde gorge close to Zahara de la Sierra (which Walk 29 explores) and numbers are being maintained thanks to various feeding sites in the high Sierra. The two circuits out from El Gastor (Walks 27 and

28) as well as the Coros circuit (Walk 24) will all get you up close to these magnificent soaring birds.

Egyptian vultures are also a common sighting while other species which are easily spotted include sparrowhawk, buzzard, hobby, kestrel, chough, rockthrush, warbler, flycatcher, martin, swallow and swift, golden oriole, black wheatear, hoopoe, little owl, nightjar, bee-eater, peregrine falcon, blue rock thrush and red-legged partridge as well as a host of small songbirds. If you'd like a list of the more common species visit www.cicerone.co.uk/803/resources

If this abundant birdlife attracts many visitors to the area, there are also more than 200 species of vertebrates in the park of which some 40 are mammals. These include ibex, mongoose, wild boar, genet, wildcat, otter, fox, badger, hares and rabbits as well as roe and red deer. If you're keen to observe ibex in the wild, sightings are pretty much guaranteed on the ascent of El Torreón (Walk 26).

LOS PUEBLOS BLANCOS

The villages of the Grazalema Park and those that lie just beyond are collectively known as *los Pueblos Blancos* or the White Villages. They contain some of Spain's most distinctive folk architecture with narrow streets of whitewashed houses with wrought iron *rejas* (window grilles) dropping steeply down the hillsides. The mountain perches of these villages are testimony to their having been built with defence in mind: this was the area of the last frontier or *frontera* between Moslem and Christian Spain.

During the Moorish period the villages in this area saw a huge expansion in population and the names of nearly all of them are of Arabic origin. Zahara takes its name from Al Zahar or orange blossom, Grazalema from Zagreb Salim – the village of the Salim clan – while Benamahoma means son of Mohammed.

But emigration, especially during the early years of the 20th century then later in the 1960s and 1970s, severely depleted the population of all of the villages in the Sierra. The case of Grazalema graphically illustrates this point: at the beginning of the 20th century its population numbered almost 14000 while today it is less than 3000.

Zahara de la Sierra is perhaps the most beautiful of the white villages thanks to its spectacular rocky perch with the Sierra del Pinar providing a beautiful backdrop (see Walk 31). Lying at the western edge of the park the village is closer to Sevilla and Cádiz and receives many visitors from both cities. The village has three small hotels as well as several restaurants (see Appendix C).

GRAZALEMA

Grazalema, at the heart of the park and close to the trailheads of several of the walks in this guide, also numbers among the most beautiful of the white villages. Many walking companies from the UK use the village as a

Evening light on almond groves during the descent towards Montejaque (Walk 19)

base for week-long hiking holidays while others pass through on village to village walks.

The village stands at 800m, directly in the lee of the Sierra del Pinar, just beyond the point where the Boyar corridor – formed by two parallel mountain ranges – narrows down which in turn funnels Atlantic weather systems inwards then upwards. This fact explains why the village receives much higher rainfall than other villages in the Sierra and the abundance of vegetation that surrounds the village: this is especially evident in the lush river valley of the Gaidovar (Walk 20 explores the valley).

Reaching the village was a hazardous journey until the early 20th century but the village did attract a number of British visitors thanks to a mention in Richard Ford's *A Handbook for Travellers in Spain and Readers at Home*. Its most famous foreign visitor, however, was British anthropologist Julian Pitt-Rivers who stayed in the village and who penned *People of the Sierra*. The inward-looking village described by Pitt-Rivers was to rapidly change with the coming of the roads: one to Zahara, another to Ronda and a third to Ubrique.

Nowadays tourism is an important part of the local economy and at weekends the village receives growing numbers of visitors, mostly from Sevilla and Cádiz. Although 20 years ago there was just one small hostel, the village now has four hotels (see Appendix C for the author's first

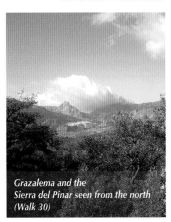

Grazalema and the Sierra del Pinar seen from the north (Walk 30)

choices) along with several bars and restaurants in and around the main square. Grazalema would be the author's first choice for a walking holiday in the area covered by this guidebook. The shop at the edge of the car park just beyond the main square sells maps of the park.

The village celebrates its annual *feria* (fair) to coincide with the feast of their patron virgin, La Virgen del Carmen, whose feast day is 16 July. During the feria, bulls are run through the streets and the tradition of the *toro de cuerda* is re-enacted when the village divides into two groups and each tries to pull a bull, roped around its horns, into their adversary's terrain.

TOURIST INFORMATION

There's a small tourist office to one side of the main car park in Grazalema but the information available is very limited. A better source of information on plants and wildlife, accommodation and walks is www.turismograzalema.info whose English web manager has been a pioneer in the promotion of all aspects of the park.

A number of shops in Grazalema sell maps and guidebooks while in Zahara de la Sierra these are also available from the small Tourist Information Point next to the village church.

PERMITS

Remember that if you plan to undertake Walks 23, 26 or 29 you'll need a permit from the Park Offices. Access to all three walks is restricted from 15 June to 1 October due to the increased risk of fire.

Permits are issued by the Park Office in El Bosque (Mon to Sat 10am to 2pm, 4pm to 6pm) where you will generally be able to get a permit for the following day if you avoid weekends and public holidays. El Bosque lies due west of Grazalema and can be reached in around 30 minutes by car.

If you don't wish to drive to El Bosque you can request permits via email: cv_elbosqueatagenciamedioambienteyagua.es

In theory the permits can also be requested by phone on 956 709 733 though it can take an age to get an answer.

You'll need to state the number of walkers, your passport number, the date and time you intend to walk and for which route you require the permit,

which can then be emailed back to you. So long as you avoid weekends and public holidays permits are generally available.

As of 2017 the Grazalema Tourist Office (see Appendix B) has been authorised to issue permits for these walks for the following day when places are available: it's worthwhile checking to save the drive across to El Bosque.

MAPS

The best maps are the IGN 1:50000 series. Walks described in this section are covered by two quadrants: 1050 Ubrique and 1036 Olvera. Another excellent map which covers the whole area is the 1:35000 Sierra de Grazalema, published by the Instituto de Cartografía de Andalucía. The Alpina 1:40000 map is a good second point of reference and includes some footpaths which aren't marked on the IGN map while, somewhat mysteriously, others are missing.

TAXI

- Grazalema: Rafael 627 415 047; Antonio 654 195 867
- Zahara: Diego 600 328 845
- El Gastor: José 659 957 083

ACCOMPANIED WALKS

The author of this book leads guided walks in the Grazalema Park. For details see www.guyhunterwatts.com

WALK 20

Grazalema northern circuit

Start/Finish	La Plaza de España, Grazalema
Distance	12.2km
Ascent/Descent	540m
Grade	Medium
Time	3hr 40min
Refreshments	None en route

This walk – a half-day outing – provides a great first taste of the beautiful valley of the Gaidovar stream that lies just to the north of Grazalema, known to locals simply as La Ribera (the river valley), and the parallel valley of the Río Guadalete.

After leaving the village via a cobbled medieval footpath that was once the main point of entry to Grazalema, a broad track leads you gently down the Guadalete valley. After crossing to its western bank a beautiful path leads on past a number of farms before you enter the next valley, La Ribera. Here you pick up another ancient section of cobbled footpath before steeling yourself for a steep climb up to the Grazalema reservoir, from where there are soaring vistas north towards Montecorto and beyond to the plateau of Acinipo – one of the major Roman settlements in the area.

From the four-spouted spring, exit the square past Bar Rumores and continue past Hotel Puerta de la Villa, then turn right then left into Calle de Arriba. The street arcs to the right before descending to a tarmac road; here turn right and after 15m go left down a cobbled footpath – the *calzada medieval* (medieval road).

Passing the last village houses, the path angles left then right before descending towards the **A-372**. Pass a sign depicting the indigenous Grazalema poppy, then go left, cross the road to a sign for 'Molinos harineros' (flour mills), and continue to descend via a concrete track that

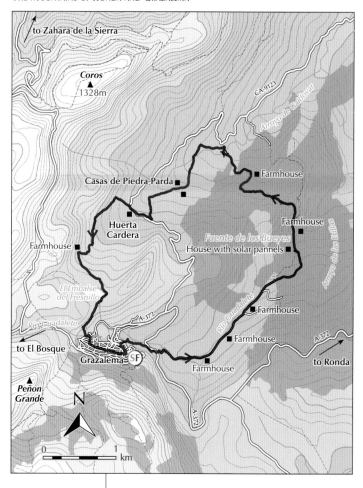

loops down into the valley where it passes a water treatment plant.

After passing **three farmhouses** the track ends at a fork. Continue straight on through a wire-and-post gate along a narrow footpath, which winds up through the oaks. The path runs up towards a low wall where you should bear left across more open ground. Over to your left, on the other side of the stream bed of the Guadalete, you'll now spot a small **white house topped by solar panels**. Using the house as your bearing, make your way down the hillside – there's no clear path at this point – to meet with a track that leads to a gap in the vegetation that lines the stream's banks.

Cross the stream (in winter and spring via stepping stones), then bearing right go through a green metal gate. The track angles up across the hillside, passing just beneath the house with solar panels. In a further 100m the track crosses a stream before reaching the spring of **Fuente de los Bueyes** which you'll see down to your right (1hr). ▶

The spring makes a natural resting point.

From the spring, retrace your steps for 10m. Continue on your former course, heading slightly up to the left, leaving the track which angles down right towards a **farmhouse**, and continue up a stony footpath. Reaching a wall, cut left for 10m then go through a black metal gate. The path climbs gently, passing above another **farmhouse** before going through a second metal gate.

Passing just left of a stone ruin, the path angles left and is marked by a series of signs for 'Cañada', which lead steeply up to a black metal gate.

Beyond the gate continue along a narrow footpath, which winds through thick undergrowth, running a few metres left of a stone wall. At a point where the wall angles left so should you, to reach a wire-and-post gate. Go through the gate and continue parallel to the wall. The path and wall angle left again and cross more open ground before re-entering thick undergrowth. Crossing the third of three stream beds, cut right to a wire-and-post gate which is opened by releasing double hooks from their rings (1hr 30min).

Beyond the gate, go right and descend between two walls. Reaching a track leading to a solitary farm, cut left and go through a wire-and-post gate 2m to the right of a metal gate. The track climbs, levels, and then descends past a number of farm sheds to reach the valley floor,

Farm track leading up from the Gaidovar valley

Grazalema's annual romería (country festivity) is sometimes held here.

where you go through another metal gate before crossing a **bridge** spanning the Arroyo de Gaidovar (marked on some maps as El Arroyo del Espinar).

Beyond the bridge follow the track over a low rise, then cut left along a less distinct track running through thick stands of broom. Angling right, it passes through a gap in a wire fence to reach a junction. Turn left, cross a stream and continue across an open tract of ground. ◄

> Nearly every village in the Ronda mountains holds an annual **romería** when the patron saint or virgin of the village is carried out into the fields close to the village where an open air mass is held. A picnic then takes place when things take on a more paganistic tone. Grazalema's romería takes place on the first fine Sunday after the middle of May.

Angling left, the track crosses the **Arroyo de Gaidovar** via a concrete bridge before passing through a gate. Just 15m beyond the gate go right at a cairn across a small olive grove, then continue up the left bank of the stream

via a cobbled footpath. Crossing to the stream's right bank via ancient stone flags, the path angles left then runs up to merge with a concrete track.

Autumnal oak in the Gaidovar valley

Passing between the houses of the farm of **Piedra Parda**, you reach a metal gate marked with the farm's name. Beyond the gate go left and continue to climb. On reaching a four-way junction where the track arcs right towards the stream, cut left up a concrete track. After passing a mill house the track narrows to become a path as it climbs between hedges, more overgrown at this stage.

> Just 50 years ago the Ribera valley was home to some 20 fulling, flour and olive **mills**, which harnessed the abundant waters running off the northern flank of the Grazalema mountains. Even though the waterwheels and millstones have long ceased to turn, a number of the original mills remain, linked by an ancient network of footpaths.

When you reach a cairn, cut right through a gap in the hedgerow into an olive grove. Bear right along the bottom

159

of the grove, parallel to the CA-9123, which you'll see up to your left. The path angles closer to the road, passes beneath twin chevrons, then runs on through the grove before meeting the **CA-9123** (2hr 30min).

Bear right along the CA-9123, then immediately beyond a bridge cut left.

Follow the track for 20m towards the entrance to **Huerta Cardera**, then go right at a fork and climb a steep concrete track. Angling left, the track climbs gently upwards before it arcs left towards a black gate. Head straight on towards a towering palm tree, cross a stream, and pass just above a farm. The path leads through a metal gate and then runs across the hillside, parallel to a wooden-posted fence. After levelling out it descends for a short distance before climbing again, narrower now, to a gate in the fence made of a rusting green bed base. Cut right through the gate, climb for 20m, then go left behind a ruined stone hut and cross a stream bed.

Peñon Grande seen on the descent from El Embalse del Fresnillo

Up above, to your right, you'll now see a **white farmhouse**. Climb up to the farmhouse, and passing 15m to its left, head left then right to reach a second farm building.

Cut left across the old threshing floor and continue along the farm's access track. After passing above an enclosure with feeders for goats, the track arcs hard right: here angle left along a narrow path towards a pylon, then pass through another bed-base gate. On reaching a low wall, go left towards another pylon, then cutting right continue along the east side of Grazalema's reservoir, **El Embalse del Fresnillo**.

Pass a small hut and drop down four flights of metal steps in front of the reservoir's retaining wall, then cross a stream, climb up through a gap in a wire fence and head left along a narrow path, following the course of a water pipe. ▶

At this stage there are fine views of Peñon Grande, towering above Grazalema.

Reach a green and white waymarking post, then 5m further on cut left down a footpath that angles right towards the village and crosses a stream via a cobbled bridge. Beyond the bridge turn left along Calle de la Asamblea, pass a small square, then cut right up Calle del Tinte Alto. Head straight across at three junctions then turn left down Calle San Jose. At the end of the street cut right, then reaching a spring go left again down Calle Las Piedras to arrive back at the village square in **Grazalema** (3hr 40min).

GRAZALEMA'S WOOL INDUSTRY

Since Berber times Grazalema has been known for the quality of its woollen goods. By the mid-19th century there was a thriving cottage industry in the village and the most tangible sign of the wealth this engendered was the building of a number of elegant three-storey houses with imposing entrances. The village took on such an air of affluence that it became known as Cádiz el Chico or Little Cádiz. There was work for the villagers in the fulling mills, spinning and carding the wool, knotting blankets, shearing sheep and transporting the merchandise.

The beginning of the 20th century saw a sudden decline in the fortunes of the village with the industrialisation of milling in the north of Spain. The cottage industry of Grazalema was no longer able to compete and most mills were forced to close. Today just one remains which makes for a fascinating visit – La Antigua Fábrica de Mantas.

WALK 21

Grazalema southern circuit

Start/Finish	Town hall, Grazalema
Distance	12.5km
Ascent/Descent	1050m
Grade	Medium/Difficult
Time	4hr 25min
Refreshments	None en route

This full-day excursion takes you to the top of two of the park's highest peaks: Simancón (1561m) and El Reloj (1535m). After a steep climb from Grazalema village (at 800m), the forested lower slopes of the Sierra del Endrinal give way to a lunar-like landscape of weathered limestone peaks. Another steep climb brings you to the top of Simancón, from where on clear days you can see all the way to Morocco and the Atlantic coast.

The path up and down El Reloj is a little trickier, but if you feel confident clambering over rocks you'll have no problem finding the way up. Bear in mind that weather conditions change rapidly in the Grazalema massif, and that the ridge linking the two peaks is very exposed. You can cut out some climbing and shorten the walk by some twenty minutes by setting out from the car park next to the campsite at the top of the village.

From in front of the town hall, leave the village square by passing right of the Unicaja bank along Calle José María Jiménez. Head left at the end of the street, then climb to the top of Calle Doctor Mateos Gago. Turn left into Calle Portal then take the next right and head up Calle Nueva, passing a spring, to the top of the village. Go left past the Fromandal cheese factory, then turn right onto the Grazalema–El Bosque road.

Cheesemaking on a commercial scale has only recently become a feature of the Sierra de

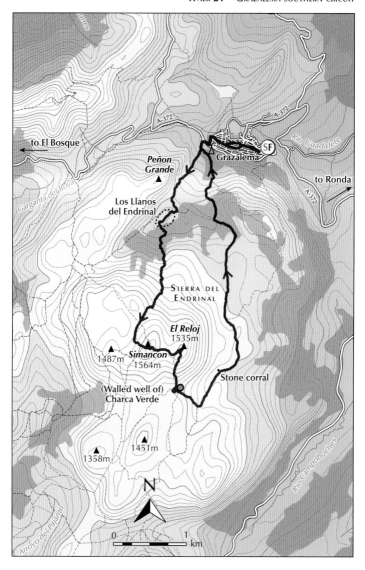

Grazalema. Following the introduction of stricter production norms after Spain's entry into the EEC, most local farmers take their milk to one of half a dozen local cheese factories. Here, as in other parts of Spain, many cheeses use a mix of ewe's, goat's and cow's milk.

After a few metres you reach a car park to the left of the road. Turn into the car park and walk along its eastern side, past the entrance to the **campsite**, to a signboard for El Complejo Subbético. Just beyond it you pick up a path to the left of a green metal gate.

The path loops left then climbs steeply up between two fences. You shortly pass through another green metal gate and continue up with the jagged ridge of **Peñon Grande** over to your right. After a steep climb through the pines the path levels then descends for about 50m to a wooden sign. Take the right-hand option, marked 'Llanos del Endrinal/Puerto del Boyar' (35min).

You shortly pass a large cairn. The path descends, crosses a flat area between the pines then arcs right before reaching an enclosure surrounded by a stone wall

Looking back to Grazalema on the ascent towards Los Llanos del Endrinal

topped by wooden posts, **Los Llanos del Endrinal**. Go left and continue along the wall's left side.

At the end of the enclosure, angling right, you come to a flat, open area. Cutting left then after 20m left again, you pick up a footpath that climbs steeply through the pines; it is overgrown in parts but easy to follow. Emerging above the tree line, the path cuts right before reaching a saddle (1hr 30min) from where you'll see Simancón's denuded massif to your left.

After angling left and running gently upwards, the indistinct path angles hard left then zigzags steeply uphill, with yellow arrows on a black background guiding you to the summit of **Simancón** (2hr 15min). ▸ To the east, connected to Simancón by a high ridge, you'll see the summit of El Reloj.

At 1561m this is the highest point on the walk.

Linked to El Reloj by a spectacular ridge of jagged karst limestone **Simancón** is the third highest peak in the province of Cádiz. The extensive panoramic view from its summit encompasses La Sierra del Pinar, La Serranía de Ronda and a huge swathe of the Parque Natural de los Alcornocales.

El Reloj seen from the summit of Simancón

Leaving the summit, drop steeply down the mountain's rocky eastern flank to the saddle linking the two mountains. Follow the ridge along, just to its right, looking for cairns. At the eastern end, reaching open, grassy ground, bear left up to the summit of **El Reloj** (1535m) (2hr 45min). From here, down in the valley floor to the south, you'll spot a circular stone wall surrounding the well at Charca Verde – your next destination.

Leave the summit by following the ridge SSW for 100m to a cairn where you head left then clamber down across the rocks, following more cairns. The path angles right, then left, to reach a flat, grassy area about the size of a tennis court. Bear left and continue to descend to the valley floor and the **walled well of Charca Verde** (3hr 10min).

Bearing left around the well, pick up a path which after 30m reaches a junction. Here cut left. A black plastic pipe crosses the path then runs just to its right and ends at a small concrete trough. The path runs on, skirting round beneath El Reloj's rocky flank, passing a sinkhole (a collapsed limestone cave) as it zigzags through low-growing oaks and pines. After running past a **stone corral** it passes through to a rickety wire-and-post gate (3hr 45min).

Eventually the path arcs down between huge rocks to reach a three-way junction. Cut right, following a sign for 'Grazalema 1.5km'. After crossing a ridge the path descends steeply back to the village campsite. Cut left long the campsite's fence to reach the path you followed earlier in the walk. Turn right, go through the green metal gate, and retrace your footsteps back to the square in **Grazalema** (4hr 25min).

WALK 22
Grazalema to Benaocáz

Start	La Plaza de España, Grazalema
Finish	Main square in Benaocáz
Distance	11.4km
Ascent	610m
Descent	640m
Grade	Medium
Time	3hr 35min
Refreshments	None en route but plenty in Benaocáz
Transport	A bus passes the end of the walk at 3.40pm (daily including Sundays). The journey back to Grazalema, passing through the pretty village of Villaluenga del Rosario, takes 30min and costs just €2.

This long and moderately challenging hike links two of the natural park's most beautiful *Pueblos Blancos* (White Villages): Grazalema and Benaocáz. The walk begins with a steep climb up to the parking area at the top of Puerto del Boyar via a broad forestry path. It's here that the walk really takes off as you gradually angle up across the western face of the Sierra del Endrinal – on a clear day you're treated to extensive views all the way down to the Atlantic coast.

After crossing a low col you descend past ancient holm oaks to the ruined farm at Casa del Dornajo where a spring runs all year round: the grassy knoll beside the spring's ancient water troughs is a superb picnic spot.

The path then winds up over a low pass before descending across a series of beautiful meadows where piles of rocks bear witness to the fact that much of this land was once cultivated.

Leave the village square in Grazalema between the Unicaja bank and the town hall along Calle José María Jiménez. Turn left at the end of the street, then passing left of house number 20 climb to the top of Calle Doctor Mateos Gago, then turn left along Calle Portal. Take the

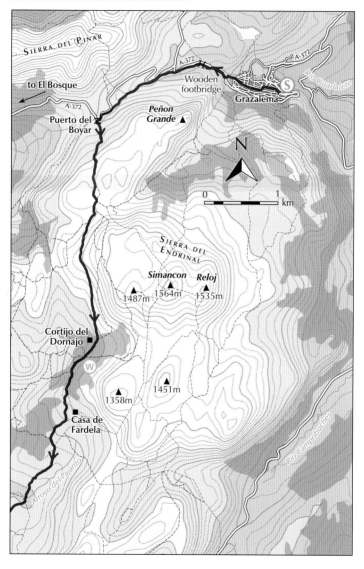

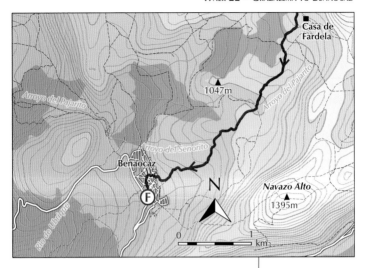

next right and continue up to the top of the village. Where the street arcs hard right towards the village cheese factory, continue straight up a narrow path that leads to the Grazalema–El Bosque/Zahara road, the **A-372**. Turn right.

A few metres before you reach a bridge across the Guadalete, cut left past a sign for Camino Peatonal, cross a **wooden footbridge** and follow a broad, sandy footpath up through an area of young pine trees. After passing a *calera* (limekiln) you arrive at the top of **Puerto del Boyar** (1103m), with a car park and the picnic area of Merendero El Boyar (55min).

Turn left along a wooden-posted fence above a spring, then pass through a metal gate and follow a rocky footpath up through the pines. After levelling and angling right past an information board the path climbs steeply once more as it passes some 50m left of another calera, which you should be able to see over to your right.

After a second steep and rocky ascent the path again levels before it passes a signboard about karrens: these sharply weathered protrusions are a typical feature of the limestone scenery in the park.

The path leading down to Cortijo Dornajo

Shortly past the sign you reach a three-way junction where a sign points left to Grazalema. Continue straight ahead and go through a gate marked 'Cierren La Puerta' (close the gate) and 'Camino Particular' (private footpath). The path angles left and descends. Angling once more right, the path climbs as it contours round the hillside with fading blue arrows marking the way.

After passing through a tumbledown wall you begin to descend, with extensive vistas opening up to the south and the Sierra de Caillo. The path gradually descends through a stand of ancient oaks before reaching the terraced land beside the ruined farm of **Cortijo del Dornajo** (1hr 50min).

The **abandoned farms** that are so much a feature of the Andalucían landscape bear testimony to the huge migratory waves to Latin America that took place in the late 19th and early 20th centuries. A second major phase of emigration, and with it a second rural exodus, took place in the 1960s and 1970s, on this occasion the destination being the factories and farms of northern Europe.

Passing left of the ruined farm, after 150m you arrive at three ancient **drinking troughs**. ▶ Leave the troughs by bearing slightly to the left and upwards. The path ascends, marked by cairns, before levelling out and then leading through a metal gate signed 'Please close the door.' From here cairns mark the path for most of the way to Benaocáz.

This is a wonderful spot to break for a rest.

Beyond the gate the path goes right and descends across a stony meadow before angling left, then once more right, to reach a larger meadow. Up ahead you'll see a stone wall – the boundary of **Casa de Fardela** (which is just out of sight beyond the wall) – but 40m before reaching the wall you bear right and head down the centre of the meadow. Cairns guide you down to a tumbledown wall topped by a metal-posted fence, where you pass through a gate made of an old bed base.

The path now arcs right and descends with a stream to its left before leading to a double set of galvanised gates. Pass through the right-hand set of gates and continue down the valley. Angling right, the path cuts through a gap in a tumbledown wall where you pass a gargantuan oak.

After crossing a stream the path angles right across an open tract of ground before passing through another bedstead gate. About 80m beyond the gate, bearing right, head on through a wire-and-post gate next to a 'Coto' sign. The path climbs gently across the meadow. ▶ After running through a more wooded area you pass through another set of twin gates; beyond the gates the path bears left then after 150m divides. Take the right fork.

The old drovers' track that once ran up the valley is partially visible over to your left.

The path broadens to become a track, which leads past a farm building before swinging right and passing through a tumbledown wall. Angling once more left, the path leads through a further set of gates before descending to reach the spring and trough of Fuente del Tejar. Turn right along a narrow path, following a sign for Nacimiento de Castril.

At the next junction turn left and drop down a cobbled path between high walls. After 30m, reaching a

The spring of Fuente del Tejar

junction in front of a high stone wall cut right, then left, then right again.

Arriving at the first village houses, turn left down Calle Villares at a sign for Barrio Nazarí and descend to Plaza Fuente Nueva. Head straight on past a No Entry sign. At the next junction turn left and continue past the village *consultorio* (medical practice) to reach the main square of **Benaocáz**, where two bars set out tables and chairs when weather permits (3hr 35min).

To reach the bus stop, head back along the street by which you entered the square. Reaching the Cajasol bank, turn left down Calle San Blas. Bearing left at Villa Soledad you reach a map of the GR7 footpath and the bus stop.

WALK 23

The Pinsapar of Grazalema

Start/Finish	Car park beside the CA-9104, 300m beyond the turning to El Bosque
Distance	11.5km
Ascent/Descent	750m
Grade	Medium/Difficult
Time	3hr 50min
Refreshments	None en route
Access	From Grazalema take the A-372 towards El Bosque then branch right on the CA-9104 for 300m towards Zahara to reach a parking area to the left of the road and the walk's start point.
Note	The walk requires a permit from the Park Office (see Grazalema introduction). It is closed between 15 June and 1 October due to the risk of fire.

The extensive stand of Spanish firs or pinsapos (*Abies pinsapo*) is the botanical jewel of the Grazalema Natural Park. The trees were first catalogued by the Swiss botanist Pierre Edmond Boissier in 1838. Smaller stands of the trees are to be found in the Sierra de las Nieves, the Sierra de Bermeja and in the Moroccan Rif, though none compares to that of Grazalema in number or extension.

This there-and back-itinerary leads you through the heart of the forest to a high pass from where you're treated to a glorious panoramic view of the northern reaches of the park. Be ready for a stiff upward climb at the beginning of both legs of the walk.

From the car park next to the A-372 exit between a hexagonal wooden hut and a signboard marking the beginning of the route. Drop down a flight of stone steps then continue past a picnic area. Pass through a black gate then follow a clear path which loops up to the top of the ridge to **Puerto de las Cumbres** (1257m) (30min). Here

173

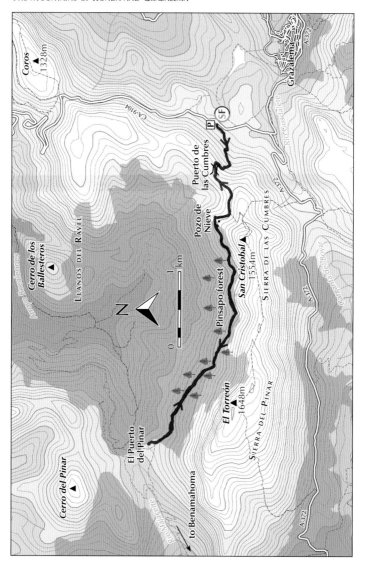

the Pinsapo forest first comes into view as views open out westwards across the park, down to the Llanos del Ravel (marked on some maps as Llanos del Revés), to the distant Sierra de Zafalgar and to the castle above Zahara.

Angling left the path contours round the northern flank of the Sierra del Pinar, at first climbing gently through gorse and hawthorn, before passing beneath the jagged peak of **San Cristobal** (1554m). Passing left of a rocky outcrop you shortly reach a signpost pointing left towards a **pozo de nieve** (ice pit). ▶

The rocky footpath beyond Puerto de las Cumbres

It's worth a 50m diversion to view one of the Sierra's best preserved of these ice pits.

Until the advent of fridges the production of ice was an important part of the local economy. Layers of packed snow were alternated with layers of broom in **ice pits**, creating a type of ice sandwich which slowed down the melting process. Blocks of ice were then wrapped in thick layers of sacking and transported on donkey or horseback as far afield as Seville and Cádiz, at a time when ice was a luxury that only the rich could afford.

Cow relaxing at El Puerto del Pinar

Continuing on west the path enters the main stand of **Pinsapo forest**, crossing a number of scree slopes before it begins to drop sharply downwards on a westerly course. The path widens as you pass a signboard about El Carboneo (the production of charcoal) as carob trees begin to appear among the fir trees. Leaving the pinsapos you reach an open, grassy area, **El Puerto del Pinar** (2hr).

It's worth climbing up its gentle western slope for soaring **views** west across the farmlands around Jerez, north towards the twin peaks of Lagarín and Las Grajas, back east across the Pinsapo forest and south to the jagged crestline of the Sierra del Pinar.

Retrace your footsteps back to the **car park** (3hr 50min).

WALK 24

*Puerto de las Palomas circuit via
the Coros peak*

Start/Finish	Car park beside Puerto de las Palomas
Distance	3.5km
Ascent/Descent	165m
Grade	Easy
Time	1hr 10min
Refreshments	None en route
Access	From Grazalema follow the A-372 then the CA-9104 towards Zahara. Reaching the top of Puerto de las Palomas park to the right of the road in a large parking area marked 'Aparcamiento Mirador'.

The mountain road linking Grazalema with Zahara de la Sierra numbers among the most spectacular in southern Spain, looping up and over the Sierra del Pinar via Puerto de las Palomas (Pass of the Doves) (1189m).

This short yet hugely rewarding walk, which is very easy to follow, begins at the car park at the top of the pass between the two villages and takes you to the top of the Coros peak (1328m) from where you're treated to a stunning 360 degree panorama that encompasses most of the Grazalema Park.

The signpost at the top of the pass indicating that you are at an altitude of 1357m is incorrect.

With your back to the sign marking Aparcamiento Mirador exit the car park by bearing left between two wooden barriers along a narrow path which after just 25m passes through a wire-and-post gate. The path angles gently upwards as views open out to the west and down to the snaking road that leads to Zahara. Soon the Zahara reservoir comes into view as the path winds clockwise round the **Coros massif**. Reaching a fork (20min) take the right-hand, higher branch and continue climbing. ▶

The mountains above Ronda and Montejaque are soon visible to the east.

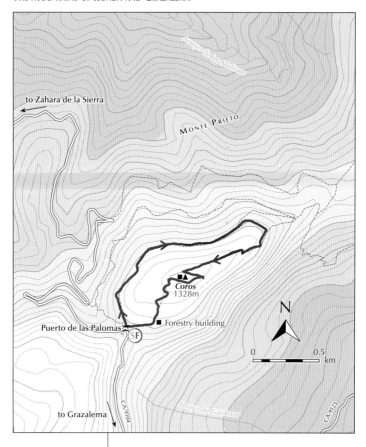

Becoming more overgrown with spikey ilex the path loops hard round to the right, running high above the path you followed earlier. Shortly, up above you to the left, you'll spot a weather station, a **white hut** and a concrete trig point. Bear sharply up left, leaving the path, and make your way up to a second trig point on the ridge top which is well to the left of the weather station (45min).

From this rocky promontory there are vast **views** which encompass the highest peaks of the Grazalema Park and several distant mountain ranges along with a number of *Pueblos Blancos* (White Villages). You're almost bound to see griffon vultures riding the thermals just above the Coros.

View across the Zahara reservoir towards the peaks of Lagarín and Las Grajas

From here head back past the weather station to a second trig point marking the highest point of the walk (1328m).

Leaving the peak pass 10m to the left of the white hut, and maintaining a course marked by a line of cairns make your way back down to the path you left earlier in the walk., Bearing left, drop down to a track that runs towards a white **forestry building**. Passing this building to its right the track runs gently down through the pines to a green gate. Some 50m beyond the gate you return to your point of departure (1hr 10min).

WALK 25
*Villaluenga circuit via
Navazo Alto and Bajo*

Start/Finish	Bus stop, Villaluenga del Rosario
Distance	8.7km
Ascent/Descent	600m
Grade	Medium/Difficult
Time	3hr 25min
Refreshments	None en route
Note	Best undertaken in dry weather because the rocky paths can be slippery after rain. Be aware that you need to take the occasional handhold due to the steepness of the paths.

Home to some of the best cheeses in the Grazalema mountains the sleepy village of Villaluenga del Rosario (872m) lies in the southern lee of the rugged massif of the Sierra del Caillo. This circuit follows a spectacular narrow, rocky footpath out from the village through a swathe of ancient terraces before angling steeply up to Puerto del Ahorcado (Pass of the Hanged Man) from where a second, beautiful section of footpath leads to the summit of Navazo Alto (1395m). Here you reap the rewards for the steep ascent: an extensive panoramic vista of the mountain ranges of the provinces of Cádiz and Málaga.

The return leg to Villaluenga is via the beautiful valley of Navazo Bajo. From here a rocky path leads steeply back down through stunning limestone formations to the village.

The walk begins in front of the bus stop at the northern edge of Villaluenga del Rosario, just beyond the Museo del Queso (cheese museum) and a children's play area. With your back to the bus stop turn right then immediately right again at a sign for Escuela de Espeleología and climb three flights of steps. Bearing left continue up past the village's unusual rectangular bullring. Reaching a fork

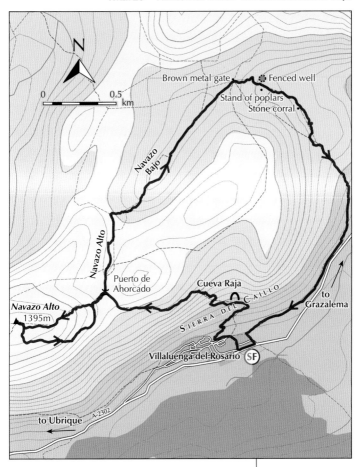

opposite the bullring's Puerta A go right and head on parallel to a stone wall and a line of street lights. Reaching recycling bins cut right and climb a narrow flight of steps in the wall. Go through a wire-and-post gate to the right of a weather station, then bearing right for 15m pass through a second gate.

Looking down to Villaluenga and its unusual octagonal bullring

CHEESEMAKING IN VILLALUENGA

Following Spain's entry into Europe laws controlling cheese production became far stricter. Faced with the high cost of equipping individual farms with the necessary equipment required under the new legislation a number of cooperatives were formed including that of Villaluenga. Over the past 15 years it has produced a number of prize-winning cheeses, using mostly a mixture of goat's and ewe's milk. Other cheese factories have sprung up and the village now hosts an annual Feria del Queso Artesanal when producers come from all over Spain to exhibit their wares. In 2016 the fair attracted more than 20,000 visitors.

Views now open out down to the village and its rectangular bullring, and out to the east towards the Sierra de Líbar.

The path angles gradually up across the hillside before looping higher it passes just beneath two wells and a drinking trough. Shortly before reaching a fence it angles hard left then passes just beneath the steep cliff face and shallow cave of **Cueva Raja**. ◄

At the far end of the cliff face take the lower, clearer branch in the footpath which leads up to a lone fig tree.

The path angles sharply right and climbs across the hillside towards a wire-and-post gate in a wall. Some 20m before you reach the gate cut sharply up left and follow the footpath steeply up to shortly pass through a wire-and-post gate (it may be open). Beyond the gate the path loops steeply upwards, then angling left over a rocky outcrop climbs at a steady gradient up to **Puerto del Ahorcado** (1240m) where you will notice a gap in a stone wall (1hr).

Just before reaching this gap bear left and climb parallel to the stone wall, which is now running just to your right. As you approach a rectangular red sign atop a rock, the path angles left, then reaching a junction after 30m cuts back right. Passing close to the sign the path climbs steeply upwards, marked by cairns. After crossing two hollows among the rocks the path runs along the left side of a third hollow then climbs for 150m to reach a junction with another path, marked by a large cairn (1hr 25min). Cut right and follow a line of cairns up to the green and white trig point atop **Navazo Alto** (1395m) (1hr 30min).

Trig point atop Navazo Alto

From the summit retrace your footsteps back to the junction with the large cairn.

Here cut right and follow the path in an easterly direction for 100m to reach another junction. Take the left fork. The path, marked by cairns, gradually angles round to the left, running across the southern flank of the Sierra del Calillo. After descending it passes above a scree slope before climbing back to reach a junction with the path you followed earlier up to the summit of Navazo Alto. Turn right and return to Puerto del Ahorcado (1hr 55min).

Here, bearing left through the wall, drop down to the flat valley floor of **Navazo Alto** (which shares its name with the peak you've just climbed). Angling 45 degrees to your right head for the lowest point on the far side of the valley. A cairn marks the continuation of the path, indistinct at first, which threads its way across a flat area between rocks, still marked by cairns. Reaching a fork at the far end of this flatter area go right. Climbing slightly the path enters a more wooded area, winding on through the oaks and rocks. Passing by a metal sign for Zona de Reserva the path begins to descend.

Some 15m before reaching a huge oak with rocks piled up at its base, bear hard right and follow a rutted path down to **Navazo Bajo** where hawthorn bushes dot the flat valley floor. Head straight up the valley, passing just to the right of a fenced enclosure. At the head of the valley the path gradually climbs, passing just left of an old bath tub serving as a drinking trough. Climbing gently up, the path reaches a wall topped by a fence and a **brown metal gate** (2hr 35min).

Cut right through the gate then follow the path which loops downhill before passing just right of a **fenced well** and a stone drinking trough. You shortly pass just to the left of a second metal drinking trough and a **stand of poplars**. Maintaining your course continue to descend for some 40m, then bearing slightly to your right the path becomes clearer, cobbled in parts, as it climbs up and over the rocks, marked by cairns.

Dropping down through the rocks the path passes just left of a large **stone corral** where to your left you'll

see three smaller corrals with metal-roofed huts. Look for a trough hollowed from a long, low rock immediately beside the footpath. Some 15m beyond the trough angle left and descend to a flat area where, angling right, the path climbs once again through the rocks. Crossing a rise it then continues its descent, looping past huge boulders, still cobbled in sections.

Eventually the path crosses a more open expanse of ground and reaches a wire-and-post gate. Beyond the gate follow the path down across the open hillside to reach another wire-and-post gate. Beyond the gate bear right along a broad, paved footpath parallel to the A-2302. Reaching the northern edge of Villaluenga take the first street to the left, then reaching the **A-2302** turn right. Passing the Museo del Queso you return to your point of departure (3hr 25min).

Approaching the summit from the south

WALK 26

Ascent of El Torreón

Start/Finish	The car park to one side of the A-372 between El Puerto del Boyar and Benamahoma
Distance	6.8km
Ascent/Descent	780m
Grade	Medium/Difficult
Time	3hr 15min
Refreshments	None en route
Access	From Grazalema follow the A-372 towards El Bosque. After crossing the pass of Puerto del Boyar continue to the parking area just before the km40 signpost.
Note	This walk requires a permit from the Park Office (see Grazalema introduction). The footpath is closed to the public between 15 June and 1 October due to the risk of fire. Be prepared for a rapid drops in temperature at the summit on cold, windy days.

At 1654m El Torreón is the highest peak in the Grazalema Park. There is just one footpath up to the summit which is clearly marked and easy to follow. The views from the top are mesmerising but be aware that just yards from the summit there are precipitous drops on the northern side of the Sierra del Pinar. You may feel safer taking the odd handhold as you clamber up and over the bare rock face on the final section of path leading to the summit, and bear in mind that the higher sections of the path can be icy during the winter months.

The chances are very good that you will spot ibex during the course of the walk; a large herd inhabit the south-facing slopes of the Sierra del Pinar.

The walk begins beside the A-372 between Grazalema and El Bosque at the car park to the left of the road. Cross the A-372 and head past a signboard marking the beginning of the route, Sendero El Torreón. From here a path leads to a fence and a green gate. Beyond the gate bear

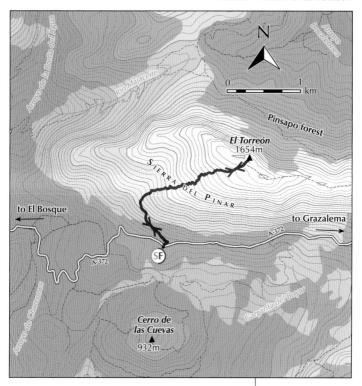

left, parallel to the fence for 75m then cut right and follow the path as it angles up across the southern face of the **Sierra del Pinar**. ▸ You climb steeply through a swathe of low-growing holly oaks, cistus, juniper, hawthorn, gorse and a few solitary pinsapos (*Abies pinsapo*, Spanish fir).

As the trees begin to thin out the path levels as you cross a flattish area among the rocks (it can be icy here in winter). After descending for 30m and crossing another hollow among the rocks, the path climbs steeply up to the summit of bare rock, marked by walker symbols, way-marking posts and cairns. At **El Torreón** summit a metal plaque tells you that you're now at 1654m (1hr 45min).

Views soon open out westwards to the Bornos reservoir and on towards the Atlantic hinterland.

187

The view west along the ridgetop of the Sierra de las Cumbres

A magnificent panorama awaits with **views** south to Gibraltar and the Moroccan Coast, Benaocáz and Ubrique, out west to Bornos, Prado del Rey and Jerez, north to the Sierra de Líjar, Olvera, Algodonales and Montecorto, while to the east Ronda and the Sierra de las Nieves are visible. On a clear day you will see the distant peaks of the Sierra Nevada way out to the east.

After taking in the views retrace your footsteps back to the walk's start point (3hr 15min).

WALK 27

El Gastor circuit via Lagarín and Las Grajas

Start/Finish	Área Recreativa La Ladera, near El Gastor
Distance	7km
Ascent/Descent	650m
Grade	Medium
Time	2hr 30min or 1hr 40min (without Las Grajas)
Refreshments	None en route
Access	From Ronda take the A-374 towards Sevilla. After 25km go right at a sign for El Gastor on the CA-9114. At 150m before the village cut right at a sign for Los Algarrobales. La Ladera picnic area is on the left after 100m.

This short but moderately demanding circuit leads you up through the pine forest above the *Pueblo Blanco* (White Village) of El Gastor to the rocky summit of Lagarín, whose plunging, south-facing cliff face is one of the region's most dramatic mountain features.

From the top of Lagarín you follow a ridge then climb to the summit of Las Grajas where more soaring vistas await.

The return leg leads back down to the village via the Dolmen del Charcón, one of the best-preserved dolmens in southern Spain. From here a steep farm track leads back to your point of departure.

With your back to the signpost marking 'Área Recreative La Ladera' turn right then after 35m cut left at a map of the village and a second one marking your route 'Tajillo/ Tajo Lagarín 3kms', then follow a steep concrete track up past the village **water deposit**. The track reverts to dirt then narrows, still climbing steeply. Some 150m past the water deposit go left through a gate made of an old pallet and follow a narrow path up through the pine forest, marked with red-arrowed waymarking.

Reaching a marker post ignore a path that angles hard right and upwards, instead maintain your course passing

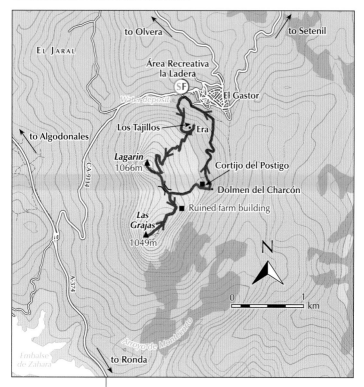

a point where a wooden barrier protects the lower side of the path. Bearing left you reach an old threshing floor or **era**. From here follow a wooden barrier just to the left of the era to reach the rocky outcrop of **Los Tajillos** (20min) from where there are views down to the village.

> The **era** or threshing platform – along with *majanos* (large piles of stones showing that the land was once cultivated) in among the pines that you pass during the ascent through the forest – bears testimony to the fact that a large part of the lower mountainside would once have been farmed.

Retrace your footsteps back to the era, then bearing across to its left follow another run of wooden-posted railing. Where these end, head sharply right and climb through the pines following red waymarking. Reaching a large cairn the path angles left, still climbing. After zig-zagging upwards you reach a junction by a huge pile of stones. Cut left, still following red waymarking. Looping higher the pines begin to thin out.

Reaching a fork (35min) in the path bear right on the higher path. ▶ Pines begin to give way to evergreen oaks as the path runs westwards beneath Lagarín's northern face before looping hard back to the left and adopting an easterly course, running just beneath a line of concrete fence posts. Reaching a fence cut right and follow it sharply upwards to reach the ridge top and a gate (55min), just above a stile (ladder) spanning the fence.

Views now open out to the east and La Sierra de las Nieves.

Here, angle 90 degrees right and follow cairns across to the massif's south-facing slope from where, bearing right and upwards through the rocks, you reach the trig point marking the summit of **Lagarín** (1066m) (1hr 5min).

The author's hat at the summit of Lagarín

At the summit a vast **panorama** awaits you, encompassing La Sierra de las Nieves, La Sierra de Grazalema, La Sierra de Líjar and La Sierra de Antequera as well as several of the Pueblos Blancos including Zahara, Algodonales, Olvera and Torre Alháquime.

Retrace your steps back to the gate in the fence at 55min next to the stile. Go through the gate then follow the ridge which descends to the **col** between Lagarín and Las Grajas. A fence runs to your right as you reach the col's lowest point and a junction (1hr 15min).

Optional ascent of Las Grajas
Here, if you wish to climb Las Grajas, maintain your course. The path threads through the rocks, close to the metal fence, then angles right towards a ladder stile. Don't cross this but rather continue along the path, still with the fence to your right. Marked by cairns the path passes to the right of a **ruined farm building** then climbs steeply to reach a second ladder stile over the fence. Climb over the fence then turn left.

Looking west to Lagarín from Las Grajas

After 40m, bearing right then back to the left, follow an indistinct path to the highest point of **Las Grajas** (1049m), close to a solitary evergreen oak at the ridge's southern edge where more extraordinary views await (1hr 45min).

Leaving Las Grajas retrace your footsteps back to the junction you passed at 1hr 15min. Turning right, you begin to descend towards El Gastor.

If you chose not to climb Las Grajas, turn left at the junction towards El Gastor. The path crosses a gentler, looping footpath five times, descending steeply towards a line of poplars. Reaching a fork cut right on a narrower path which runs down towards an evergreen oak and a picnic bench. Angling once more right you reach the **Dolmen del Charcón** (2hr 10min).

> The **Dolmen del Charcón**, also known locally as the Dolmen del Gigante, is a megalithic burial chamber some 6000 years old. It measures 8.5m in length, 1.5m in width and 1.5m in height. When the tomb was first excavated in 1975 arrow heads and pottery shards were found within the main chamber and are assumed to have formed part of funerary offerings.

From the dolmen angle down a lower path which descends towards the line of poplars. After 40m the path merges with a track which passes beneath the ruins of the **Cortijo del Postigo** then runs through a grove of poplars. Passing through a green metal gate the track loops right then left, crosses a cattle grid then passes through a second gate. Reaching a junction with a dirt track next to a sign for Dolmen del Charcón follow it left for 450m to return to your point of departure (2hr 30min).

WALK 28
El Gastor circuit via Huerta Lagarín

Start/Finish	Área Recreativa la Ladera, near El Gastor
Distance	8.4km
Ascent/Descent	300m
Grade	Medium
Time	2hr 5min
Refreshments	None en route
Access	From Ronda take the A-374 towards Sevilla. After 25km go right at a sign for El Gastor on the CA-9114. 150m before the village cut right at a sign for Los Algarrobales. La Ladera picnic area is on the left after 100m.

This short and easy-to-follow circuit, by way of broad farm tracks, offers memorable views at every turn, and leads you all the way round the lower slopes of Lagarín and Las Grajas.

The peaks' spectacular south-facing cliff faces are home to a large colony of griffon vultures (*Gyps fulvus*) whose display of aerial mastery helps make this an absolute must-walk. You may also spot ibex on the rocks high above you. Binoculars will increase your enjoyment of this walk which is classed Medium rather than Easy because of one very steep section of climbing about halfway round the mountain.

Groves of olives give way to extensive stands of carob and broom as views open out eastwards towards the Sierra de Ronda then south towards the Grazalema mountains.

Facing a signboard for Vuelta al Tajo Lagarín depicting the route you'll be following from La Ladera, which is signed by blue-banded marker posts, cut left and follow a track through the pine forest. Ignore a track that cuts right at a sign for Dolmen del Charcón. Reaching a junction of four tracks turn right following a sign for Los Algarrobales.

The track descends gently, following a line of pylons, passing first the entrance gate of **Los Algarrobales** then a second set of gates topped by twin eagles leading to **El Paraiso Escondido**. ◀

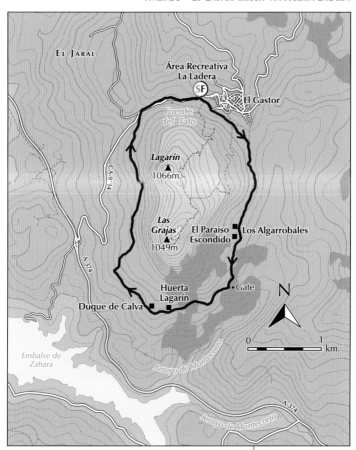

Reaching a metal **gate** marked 'Huerta Lagarín' cut left, pass through a smaller wire-and-post gate, then rejoin the track which continues to descend, contouring gradually round beneath the rocky eastern flank of Las Grajas. Reaching a second set of gates, some 75m before the farmhouse of **Huerta Lagarín**, pass through a smaller metal gate just to their left (55min).

Looking north towards Las Grajas

Running on past a wall made of huge boulders, then passing just left of the farmhouse, the track crosses an old threshing floor, passes a spring (sometimes dry) before reaching a second set of metal gates. Passing just right of the gates, exit the farm via a smaller metal gate. Continue along the track which shortly passes beneath the entrance to the farm of **Duque de Calva** as vast views open out across the reservoir to Zahara de la Sierra and its Moorish castle.

Reaching a fork just beyond a blue-banded marker post go right, sticking to the main track which now begins to climb very steeply towards the southern flank of Las Grajas. Passing a 20km speed limit sign, the track bears left and levels.

Reaching a fork just beyond a sign for Huerta Lagarín pointing back the way you've come, take the right-hand option. The track, concrete in sections, runs on to the west as it passes beneath the steep cliff face of Lagarín. The track turns to tarmac before it reaches a junction with the **CA-9114**. Cross the road then cut right along a flagged footpath following a sign for 'El Gastor 1.2km'.

The path leads past a group of three white houses then the **Fuente del Gato**. Some 75m beyond the spring cut right at a sign for Los Algarrobales to return to your point of departure (2hr 5min).

WALK 29

The Garganta Verde

Start/Finish	Car park beside the CA-531, 4km from Zahara
Distance	5.5km
Ascent/Descent	350m
Grade	Medium
Time	2hr 5min
Refreshments	None en route
Access	From Zahara de la Sierra take the CA-531 towards Grazalema for 4km. The car park and start point are to the right of the road marked by a blue sign, 'Sendero Garganta Verde'.
Note	This walk requires a permit from the Park Office (see Grazalema introduction). The footpath is closed to the public between 15 June and 1 October because of the risk of fire.

The descent into the plunging gorge of the Garganta Verde (Green Gorge) numbers among the Grazalema Park's most stunning on-foot adventures. The gorge is home to a large colony of griffon vultures (*Gyps fulvus*) and there's nowhere like here for close-up observation of the huge raptors which take to the wing once the morning thermals begin to rise.

Early in the walk you follow a narrow path that cuts along the gorge's northern flank past a series of the vultures' rocky perches before zigzagging steeply down to reach the open-sided cavern known to locals as La Ermita (The Chapel). This towering amphitheatre is best seen when the mid-morning sunlight strikes its rosy-coloured overhang, cloaked in delicate stalactites in pastel-pinks and greens. This is a spot to be savoured and a perfect place to break for a picnic before you tackle the steep climb back to the walk's start point.

Leave the car park past a signboard with a map of the route that you're about to follow marked 'Sendero Garganta Verde, SLA118'. Descend a flight of steps and

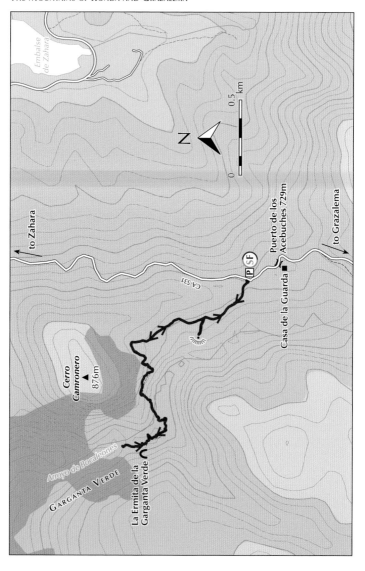

Embalse
de Zahara

0.5 km

N

0

to Zahara

CA-531

P SF

Puerto de los
Acebuches 729m

to Grazalema

Casa de la Guarda

Cerro
Camronero
876m

Arroyo de Bocaleones

GARGANTA VERDE

La Ermita de la
Garganta Verde

pass through a black gate. The path cuts right, adopting a fairly level course as it contours high along the gorge's northern flank. Reaching a sign for a **mirador**, and cutting left for a few metres you reach a rocky promontory with soaring views out across the gorge.

> The **Garganta Verde** or Green Gorge takes its name from the abundant vegetation that cloaks its high cliff faces. The gorge, gouged out of the limestone and dolomite of the Sierra Cambronero by the Arroyo del Pinar, plunges to 400m at its deepest point. With specialist equipment it's possible to descend the section of the gorge that lies beyond La Ermita: this involves abseiling down four waterfalls.

A group departs to abseil down the waterfalls lower down the gorge

The rocky riverbed next to La Ermita

From the Ermita you can continue for approximately 150m to a point where you reach the first of a series of waterfalls (dry for most of the year) whose descent requires abseiling down three of them.

Retrace your steps back to the path which now runs uphill for a few hundred metres, threading its way through gorse, lentiscus and fan palms before angling back towards the gorge. Passing two tumbledown corrals it loops steeply downwards, with some sections protected by metal barriers. Reaching the base of the gorge and the bed of the **Arroyo de Bocaleones** the path angles right between boulders before leading you down to the stunning natural amphitheatre of **La Ermita de la Garganta Verde** (55min). ◀ Retrace your steps back to the start point of the walk (2hr 5min).

WALK 30
Algodonales circuit via El Canalizo

Start/Finish	Área Recreativa los Nacimientos
Distance	8.5km
Ascent/Descent	550m
Grade	Medium
Time	3hr
Refreshments	None en route
Access	From Ronda take the A-374 towards Sevilla then the A-382 towards Olvera. Go left at km post 83 then follow the track for 1km to reach the Área Recreativa los Nacimientos.
Note	Sections of the footpath are slightly overgrown so this is a walk best undertaken in long trousers.

This superb half-day hike explores the eastern side of the Sierra de Líjar and the majestic beauty of the Arroyo del Nacimiento gorge, known to locals as El Canalizo. At first the path hugs the stream bed before looping sharply up to the Líjar massif's southern face. Here the Mirador de las Víboras (754m) offers soaring views out across the Zahara reservoir.

A short section of forestry track then leads to the Fuente de las Víboras – it may well be dry – before a mesmerisingly beautiful path loops round the upper reaches of the Nacimiento gorge, eventually crossing the stream high up the Canalizo before climbing to the top of the Líjar plateau. An easy and well-marked footpath leads back to Los Nacimientos.

The walk begins at the entrance posts to the Área Recreativa los Nacimientos. From here head past picnic benches and a group of palm trees, climb through a barred green metal gate to the left of a larger gate then after 40m cut right up a narrow footpath. After bearing right then once more left the path runs parallel to a fence before looping back and forth across the stream bed of the **Arroyo del Nacimiento**, passing through stands of

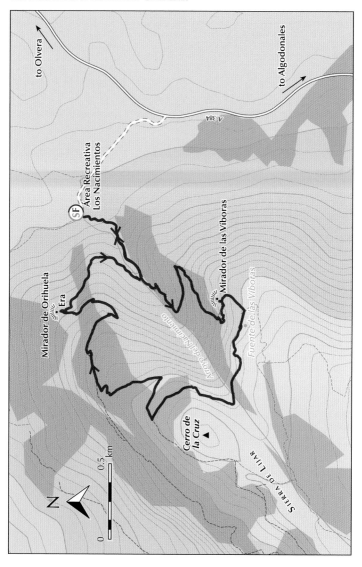

carob and wild olive. After 600m you reach a fork in the path (15min) and a marker post pointing right to La Muela.

Here cut left onto a narrower footpath which climbs in a series of loops. ▶

After climbing, the path angles hard left then runs in a more westerly direction to reach a rocky outcrop where angling right it adopts its former course. After zigzagging more steeply upwards you pass a wooden barrier. A series of rocky steps then leads you up to another limestone outcrop and the **Mirador de las Víboras**, just to the left of the footpath (1hr 5min).

Beyond the mirador the path, now more overgrown, climbs through low-growing vegetation to reach a track. Turning right after 150m you reach the water deposit of the **Fuente de las Víboras**. Some 5m before you reach a smaller water deposit with a green metal door, bear left up a narrow, indistinct path. It soon becomes clearer as its climbs gradually up through stands of wild olive, shortly

The footpath beside the Arroyo del Nacimiento

Views open out across to the rocky outcrops at the higher reaches of the Canalizo gorge where griffon vultures will nearly always be riding the thermals.

203

passing through a breach in the rocks. Running on across the hillside its cuts across the stream bed of the **Arroyo del Nacimiento**. Ignore another path that cuts left just before you reach the stream bed. Angling hard to the right the path shortly crosses over a field of rock where, maintaining your course, you pick up the footpath once again.

The path becomes more spectacular as it passes beneath a high rock face with a deep, ochre-coloured depression. Just beyond this rock face, looping up to a higher level, it runs towards a breach in the rock from where Olvera is visible. Keeping left of this breach the path climbs to reach the top of the Líjar plateau where it becomes more overgrown.

Reaching a junction (1hr 50min) and a wooden marker post, cut right along a better defined footpath. Running up to meet a fence the path angles hard left before looping back round to the right, now adopting a more northerly course before coming to a junction with another path. Turn right following a sign for 'Área Recreativa los Nacimientos, 2.5kms'. Passing a stone bench you come to the **Mirador de Orihuela** from where the elephantine outcrop of El Peñon de Zaframagón is visible to the north.

> The spectacular outcrop (*peñon*) of **Zaframagón**, formed of dolomite during the Jurassic period, can be accessed via the Via Verde (or cycle path) that leads from Olvera west towards Jerez. It is home to one of the largest colonies of griffon vultures in southern Spain.

From the mirador the path zigzags down to a cobbled **era** (threshing floor). Follow along the right side of the era. Cutting right then left between two carob trees you pick up the continuation of the path. After running in a more easterly direction the path angles gradually right before descending and crossing the **Arroyo del Nacimiento** once again. Bearing once more left you reach the junction that you passed at 15min.

Retrace your footsteps back down to the **Área Recreativa los Nacimientos** (3hr).

WALK 31
Zahara de la Sierra circuit

Start/Finish	Town hall, Zahara de la Sierra
Distance	14.5km
Ascent/Descent	750m
Grade	Medium/Difficult
Time	4hr 10min
Refreshments	None en route
Note	There is prickly gorse on the first part of the Parralejo ascent so consider putting a pair of long trousers in your daypack.
Warning	This walk is not recommended after heavy rain, when crossing the Parralejo can become tricky.

This memorable circular route begins and ends in one of the *Pueblos Blancos* (White Villages), Zahara de la Sierra, at the western fringe of the Grazalema Park.

The walk begins with a steep descent from the village to the Arroyo del Bocaleones. From here you cross open farmland before cutting south to pick up the course of the Arroyo del Parralejo, where you begin a long but gradual climb up to the Breña pass, the last section through a wonderful expanse of *dehesa* (forest which has been partially cleared to leave selected species eg evergreen and cork).

Descending from the pass you have fine views across the valley towards the mouths of the Garganta Seca and the Garganta Verde. These spectacular gorges are home to one of Europe's largest colonies of griffon vultures and you're almost guaranteed fine sightings of these soaring raptors on this walk. The walk ends with a steep pull up through olive groves back to the village so save a bit of extra puff for this section.

Exit the square to the left of the town hall of Zahara de la Sierra, following a sign for Salida. Go right at the first fork then turn left into Calle Peñas. At the end of the street, just past the second of two houses marked '33', bear right and descend past a sign for Príncipe Felipe.

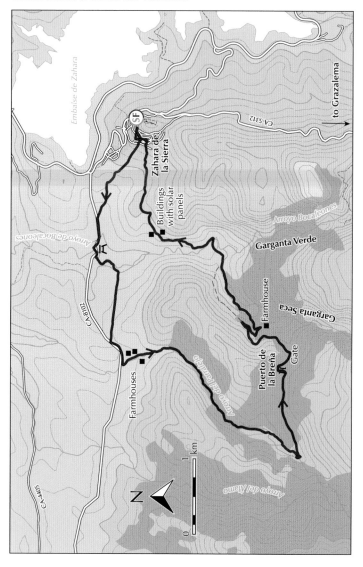

On reaching a pedestrian crossing by a palm tree, cross the road and turn left then immediately right down a concrete track, following a line of wooden telegraph poles.

The concrete ends as the track swings left to a green gate. Don't go through the gate, but instead continue straight down an eroded dirt track. The track angles right to a junction with a concrete road where turning left you descend to meet with a tarmac road (20min).

Turn left and follow the **CA-8102** for 500m where after heading right then left it crosses the Arroyo de Bocaleones at a **picnic area**. Just as you reach a chevron between you and the picnic area bear left away from the road. Passing 15m left of a line of recycling bins follow a narrow footpath that soon merges with another that runs beside a water channel. Reaching a sluice gate cross the channel, then bearing left continue parallel to the Arroyo de Bocaleones.

The path merges with a track that runs down towards a stand of eucalyptus and the stream: ignore the track and instead continue parallel to the stream's right bank.

Zahara and its Moorish castle seen from the west

207

Reaching a second stand of eucalyptus cut left along a narrow path close to the stream. On reaching more open ground the path merges with a track. Follow the track for 70m then cut right at a cairn with waymarking stripes. Head steeply up the right bank of a stream and after 80m you'll reach a fence. Cut steeply up to your right, then left, then continue along a dirt track – gravelled in parts – that climbs between fences. Maintaining a westerly course you drop back down to the CA-8102 which you left earlier in the walk.

Turn left and follow the road for 350m. Just before a small bridge with metal barriers, turn left along a dirt track. After passing two **farmhouses** you reach a third. Head straight on, passing the farmhouse to your right. The track narrows to become a path. Follow the path, indistinct at times but marked with cairns, gently upwards, parallel to the course of the stream bed of the **Arroyo del Parralejo**. Soon you pass through a wire-and-post gate (50min).

Continue along the left bank of the stream, looking for cairns. Eventually the path cuts right and left, then passes through a gate signed 'Coto Privado de Caza' (private hunting reserve) (1hr 15min). A few metres beyond the gate you cross the stream for the first time. Bearing left, after 15m cross back to the left bank. A fence now runs to your left; where the fence angles left, cross the stream once more then angle back again to its left bank. Crossing the stream for a fifth time, the path divides: take the right fork and continue over a low rise – taking care, as there are steep drops to your left – then cross back to the left bank of the stream.

After 5m you reach a wire-and-post gate next to a black and white 'Coto' sign. Don't go through this gate but instead pass just to its right. Continuing parallel to a fence to your left for 30m cross the dry stream bed once again. Bearing left you pass right of a huge oak then a small, circular enclosure to reach a gate made of an old bed base. Go through the gate then angle left, cross the stream bed once again then drop down over a tumble-down wall into a large enclosure with deciduous oaks. Turn right: the stream and a wall are now to your right.

Sticking close to the wall head gently up to the far end of the enclosure. Bearing left, you climb a steep bank then meet with a broad forestry track. Turning left, follow the track up to **Puerto de la Breña**, where you'll see a stone circle to your left where helicopters can land (2hr 5min). ▶

Beyond the pass the rocky defiles of the Garganta Seca and the Garganta Verde, across the valley, come into view.

Resident colonies of **griffon vultures** (*Gyps fulvus*), one of Europe's largest raptors, inhabit the steep cliffs of both the Garganta Verde (green gorge) and the Garganta Seca (dry gorge). Access to both gorges is prohibited during the summer months, and at other times of the year a permit is required.

The track bears left, descends and passes through a green metal **gate**. Ignore a first track cutting down to the right after just over 800m. Continue for some 20min to reach a junction, where a track angles hard right, down towards a **farm** that you'll have spotted on your descent from La Breña. At a sign for Zona de Seguridad (security zone), turn hard right and descend to a black metal gate.

Immediately beyond the gate turn left along a narrow path. Cairns and faded green markers indicate the route,

Footpath on the descent towards the Arroyo de Bocaleones

In the warmer months it's worth cutting right just beyond the stream and then cutting right again when you reach a metal gate. A narrow path leads to a pretty bathing spot between the rocks.

which eventually leads through a gate made of an old bed base before meeting with the track you left higher up the valley. Bearing right and descending, the track crosses the **Arroyo de Bocaleones** (2hr 55min). ◄

Beyond the stream the track bears left past the gates of Los Laureles, then climbs steeply through olive groves. Passing **two buildings with solar panels**, it levels before descending to a whitewashed farm where the track angles left towards a green gate.

Just before you reach the gate, cut right up a path that climbs steeply up the edge of an olive grove, loops across a gully then merges with a concrete track.

Reaching a junction, turn left past Molino La Ermita then cut right past a No Entry sign. After passing a children's nursery the road bears left and reaches a junction by a pedestrian crossing. Go left across the road past Constructora Zahara Sierra, and follow this road back up to the square in **Zahara de la Sierra** (4hr 10min).

ZAHARA DE LA SIERRA

Zahara de la Sierra was once known as Zahara de los Membrillos or Zahara of the Quince Trees at a time when there were extensive, cultivated groves just beneath the village. The village dates from the Moorish period when the Berber settlement was further up the hill behind the church in the central square, clinging to the hillside beneath its castle. It was only after it had been reconquered by the Christians that the village expanded beyond the walls along what is now its main street.

Zahara is known throughout Spain for its remarkable Corpus Christi celebrations. Every year, on the day before Corpus, the villagers cut down oleander, reeds, mimosa, eucalyptus and palm fronds – indeed, anything which is green – and set about covering the facades of the houses and streets of the village. A white village, overnight becomes a green one.

WALK 32

Benamahoma circuit

Start/Finish	Área Recreativa los Llanos del Campo, near Benamahoma
Distance	7km
Ascent/Descent	250m
Grade	Easy
Time	1hr 50min
Refreshments	None en route
Access	From Grazalema follow the A-372 towards El Bosque. After crossing Puerto del Boyar continue to the parking area to the right of the road at km 37.
Note	The cairns on the middle part of the walk are sometimes knocked down by cattle. Please add to those you come across.

This easy circular walk, which begins at a picnic area just a few kilometres east of the pretty village of Benamahoma on the southern side of the Sierra del Pinar, could make for a gentle introduction to the great natural beauty of the Grazalema Park.

After following the ancient cobbled footpath that once connected Grazalema with the white villages further to the west, you cut across the A-372 before returning to your departure point by way of an ancient path that winds through moss-covered rocks, passing by ancient carobs, holm and gall oaks.

The walk starts in the car park of the Área Recreativa los Llanos del Campo. From the car park's western edge pass through a green metal gate and head to the far end of a small football pitch where you pass a signboard for Arroyo del Descansadero. Maintain your course past a group of picnic benches, close to the **A-372**, then pass through a second metal gate. Beyond the gate turn right following a sign for Área Recreativa.

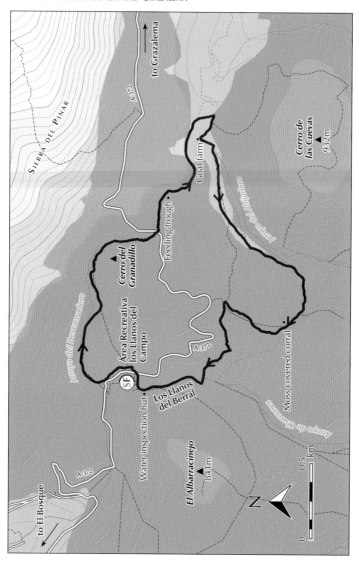

The path, cobbled in parts, climbs gradually through deciduous and evergreen oaks, parallel to the right bank of the **Arroyo del Descansadero**. Reaching a junction with a path that arcs hard right, maintain your course. ▶ Cutting up right then once more left the path becomes narrower and less distinct. After widening again, where cobbling is again visible, the path angles right, occasionally braiding, as it runs through boulders and oaks to reach a wire-and-post gate (35min).

Beyond the gate cross the **A-372** then climb through a swinging gate just left of a larger one marked 'Zona de Seguridad'. Continue along a broad gravel track. After passing a **feeding trough** the track gradually bears right as views open out southwards, running past huge boulders and ancient oak and carob trees. After passing above a **goat farm** the track divides. Take the right-hand track which loops harder right before descending towards the goat farm.

Just before reaching the farm the track angles hard left and ends. Hold your course across an area of open meadow. Reaching its far end, cut right. The path becomes clearer as it runs on, passing just to the right of two eucalyptus trees. Beyond the trees the path, clearer now, begins to descend. Look out for cairns. Levelling, it crosses another dry stream bed then braiding occasionally runs across more open ground. Beyond this clearing the path bears slightly left, now running parallel to the stream bed of the **Arroyo del Ahijadero** which is down to your left. Again the path braids but soon becomes clearer, passing an unusually formed oak whose trunk runs for 4m parallel to the ground before rising upwards.

The path climbs gradually as it bears round to the right and northwards, winding through boulders and trees cloaked in mosses and ferns, before running across another flat swathe of meadow. Passing right of an enormous oak the path braids as it reaches a **moss-covered corral**. Take the path closest to the corral. The path now heads right, climbing gently upwards to reach a junction with a clearer path. Turn left (1hr 25min).

To your left the southern slopes of the Sierra del Pinar rise majestically upwards.

The old path that climbs from Los Llanos del Campo

Winding down through rocks, oaks and carob you reach a flat, open area where there are abandoned olives, **Los Llanos del Berral**. Maintaining your course past the first of the olives, hung with a rectangular red sign, cross a stream bed. After 100m you reach a cairn. Bear hard left to reach a forestry track and a signboard for La Vegetación Mediterránea. Cut right and follow the track back towards the A-372. Some 50m past a **water inspection hut** the track angles hard right. Reaching a marker post topped with a white arrow go right, away from the track, along a path that leads to a green gate. Beyond the gate cross the **A-372** to return to your point of departure (1hr 50min).

APPENDIX A
Route summary table

No	Start	Grade	Distance	Ascent/Descent	Time	Page
Ronda and the Sierra de las Nieves						
1	Puerto de Caucón	Medium	7km	475m	2hr 10min	40
2	Puerto del Saucillo	Medium/Difficult	12.5km	800m	4hr	45
3	Los Sauces	Medium/Difficult	14.7km	800m	4hr 15min	50
4	El Burgo	Medium	14km	375m	3hr 45min	56
5	Los Queijgales	Difficult	15.7km	975m	5hr 15min	61
6	Ronda	Easy/Medium	6km	240m	1hr 40min	68
7	Ronda	Medium	14km	375m	3hr 35min	73
8	Ronda	Easy	4.5km	125m	1hr 30min	77
The Genal and Guadiaro Valleys						
9	Cartajima	Medium/Difficult	15.5km	750m	4hr 20min	90
10	Cartajima	Medium/Difficult	13.5km	800m	4hr	96
11	Alpandeire	Easy/Medium	3.8km	225m	1hr 15min	102
12	Estación de Benaoján	Easy	8.5km	45m/140m	2hr	106
13	Estación de Benaoján	Easy	7.7km	250m	2hr 5min	110
14	Estación de Jimera	Medium	11km	150m	3hr	114

No	Start	Grade	Distance	Ascent/Descent	Time	Page
15	Cortes de la Frontera	Difficult	13km	875m	5hr	119
16	Cortes de la Frontera	Medium	12.7km	475m	3hr 15min	125
17	Benarrabá	Medium/Difficult	13km	890m	4hr 10min	131
18	Gaucín	Medium	11.8km	630m	2hr 50min	137
19	Montejaque	Medium/Difficult	16.3km	710m	4hr 55min	142
The Sierra de Grazalema						
20	Grazalema	Medium	12.2km	540m	3hr 40min	155
21	Grazalema	Medium/Difficult	12.5km	1050m	4hr 25min	162
22	Grazalema	Medium	11.4km	610m/640m	3hr 35min	167
23	Between Grazalema and Zahara	Medium/Difficult	11.5km	750m	3hr 50min	173
24	Puerto de las Palomas	Easy	3.5km	165m	1hr 10min	177
25	Villaluenga del Rosario	Medium/Difficult	8.7km	600m	3hr 25min	180
26	Close to El Puerto del Boyar	Medium/Difficult	6.8km	780m	3hr 15min	186
27	El Gastor	Medium	7km	650m	2hr 30min	189
28	El Gastor	Medium	8.4km	300m	2hr 5min	194
29	Close to Zahara	Medium	5.5km	350m	2hr 5min	197
30	Los Nacimientos	Medium	8.5km	550m	3hr	201
31	Zahara de la Sierra	Medium/Difficult	14.5km	750m	4hr 10min	205
32	Los Llanos del Campo	Easy	7km	250m	1h 50min	211

APPENDIX B
Useful contacts

Note: Many of the websites listed below are in Spanish by default, but most include the option of an English-language version at the click of a button.

Transport

Train
Renfe (national rail operator)
tel (+34) 902 320 320
www.renfe.com

Buses

Ex-Málaga and Sevilla
Autocares Los Amarillos
www.samar.es

Ex-Jerez
Autocares Comes
www.tgcomes.es

Car Rental Agencies
All major car hire companies are present in Málaga and Sevilla and several also operate out of Jerez.

Ronda
Auto Ronda Rentacar
Calle Genal 26
29400 Ronda
tel 952 879 097

Tourist information

Ronda
Oficina de Turismo
Paseo de Blas Infante
29400 Ronda
www.turismoderonda.es
tel 952 187 119

Grazalema
Oficina de Turismo
Plaza de los Asomaderos s/n
10h-15h, 15h-17.30h Tues-Sun
http://turismograzalema.com/english
tel 956 132 052

Montejaque
Oficina de Turismo
Avenida de Andalucía 45
www.montexaquez.org (Spanish)
tel 651 304 141

El Bosque
Centro de Visitantes
Calle García Lorca 1
tel 956 709 733
cv_elbosqueatagenciamedioambient
eyagua.es

Maps

In Andalucía
LTC
Avenida Menéndez Pelayo 42–44
Sevilla
www.ltcideas.es/index.php/mapas

Mapas y Compañia
Calle de la Compañía, 33
29008 Málaga
www.mapasycia.es

In Madrid

La Tienda Verde
Calle Maudes 23 and 28
28003 Madrid
www.tiendaverde.es

Centro Nacional de Información
Geográfica
General Ibáñez de Ibero 3
28003 Madrid
www.cnig.es

Desnivel
Plaza Matute 6
28012 Madrid
www.libreriadesnivel.com

In the UK

Stanfords
12–14 Long Acre
London
WC2E 9LP
www.stanfords.co.uk

The Map Shop
15 High Street
Upton upon Severn
www.themapshop.co.uk/

Birdwatching and wildlife

www.andaluciabirdsociety.org
The Andalucía Bird Society is a great
first stop for anybody interested in the
birdlife of the area.

www.spanishnature.com
Spanish Nature provide organised
birding tours and walks in Andalucía
and further afield.

www.iberianatureforum.com
The Iberia Nature Forum provides
comprehensive information, news and
discussion about the plants and wildlife
of the region.

Emergency services

Emergency services (general)
112

Guardía Civil (police)
062

Local police
092

Medical emergencies
061

Fire service
080

British Consulate General (Madrid)
tel 917 146 300

APPENDIX C
Accommodation

The following price ranges are intended as a guideline only. You may find lower prices out of season or by shopping around on the internet.

€less than €50 for a double room
€€between €50 and €75 for a double room
€€€more than €75 for a double room

Ronda and the Sierra de las Nieves

Tolox
Hotel Cerro de Hijar €€-€€€
Huge rooms and excellent food high above Tolox
www.cerrodehijar.com

Alozaina
Hostal Sango Sierra de las Nieves €
Cheap and cheerful rooms with a bar serving tapas down below
www.sangosierradelasnieves.com

El Burgo
La Casa Grande del Burgo €€
Cosy small hotel in the centre of the village
www.hotel-lacasagrande.com

Ronda
Hotel San Gabriel €€€
Characterful hotel at the heart of the old town
www.hotelsangabriel.com

Alavera de los Baños €€€
Quiet hotel next to the Arab baths at the edge of the old town
www.alaveradelosbanos.com

Hotel San Francisco €€
Spruce little hotel in a quiet street in the centre of town
www.hotelsanfrancisco-ronda.com

Hotel Montelirio €€€
Superb rooms in a 17th-century mansion at the edge of the town's famous gorge
www.hotelmontelirio.com

Close to Ronda
Finca Los Pastores €€€
Converted cortijo in an idyllic setting 5km south of Ronda
www.fincalospastores.com

Hotel Fuente de la Higuera €€€
Stylish and secluded hotel with superb rooms and top-notch food
www.hotellafuente.com

The Genal and Gaudiaro Valleys

Alpandeire
La Casa Grande €€
A quiet, village centre hotel with excellent food and rooms
www.hotelcasagrande.es

Júzcar

Hotel Bandolero €€
Smurf-blue hotel with great food and
friendly management
www.hotelbandolero.com

Cartajima

Hotel Los Castaños €€€
Cosy hotel in the village centre with
excellent cuisine
www.loscastanos.com

Montejaque

La Posada del Fresno €€
Cosy village inn with simple rooms and
friendly owners
www.posadadelfresno.com

Close to Montejaque

Hotel Cortijo las Piletas €€€
Superb rooms in a converted cortijo
between Ronda and Montejaque
www.cortijolaspiletas.com

Benaoján Estación

Hotel Molino del Santo €€€
Great food and rooms beside a rushing
mountain torrent
www.molinodelsanto.com

Jimera de Líbar

Hotel Inz Almaraz €
Quiet village hotel, exceptional value
for both food and rooms
www.hotelinzalmaraz.com

The Sierra de Grazalema

Grazalema

Hotel Casa de las Piedras €€
Simple hotel and restaurant in the
village centre
www.casadelaspiedras.es

La Mejorana €€
Superb B&B with garden, pool and
lovely views
www.lamejorana.net

Near Grazalema

Tambor del Llano €€€
Enchanting, isolated rural hotel at the
heart of the park
www.tambordelllano.es

Zahara de la Sierra

Hotel Al Lago €€€
Great food and stylish rooms with views
out to the Zahara reservoir
www.al-lago.es

Hotel Los Tadeos €€
Friendly hotel on the outskirts of the
village with a huge pool and great
views
www.alojamientoruralcadiz.com

APPENDIX D
Glossary

arroyo	stream
ayuntamiento	town hall
bodega	winery
calera	limekiln
caña	bamboo-type plant
cañada	public footpath or drovers' route
cortijo	farm
consultorio	doctor's surgery
coto (de caza)	hunting reserve
dehesa	forest which has been partially cleared to leave selected species eg evergreen and cork
era	threshing floor
fuente	spring
GR	abbreviation for Gran Recorrido or long-distance Footpath
karren	area of exposed limestone to which dissolution imparts a pavement-like appearance
karst	deeply weathered landscape formed by the action of rain-
fall	and the subsequent acidic dissolution of soluble rock like limestone, dolomite and gypsum
majano	large pile of stones, a testimony that the land around it was once under cultivation
mirador	viewing point
Mozarabic	relating to Christian inhabitants living in Spain during the Moorish period
nava	large flat expanse of land between surrounding outcrops, a typical feature of limestone scenery
pinsapo	Spanish fir, Abies pinsapo
pozo de hielo	ice pit
puerto	mountain pass
PR	abbreviation for Pequeño Recorrido or short-distance footpath
romería	country festivity following an open air mass

APPENDIX E
Further reading

Plants and wildlife
A good field guide to both the birds and flowers of the area will enrich any walk in Andalucía. The better-known field guides, which are nearly all easily available in the UK and via the internet, include the following:

Botanical Guides
Marjorie Blamey and Christopher Grey-Wilson, *Wildflowers of the Mediterranean*, A&C Black, 2004

Davies and Gibbons, *A Field Guide to the Wild Flowers of Southern Europe*, The Crowood Press Ltd, 1993. A comprehensive work of manageable size.

Betty Molesworth Allen, *Wildflowers of Southern Spain*, Santana Books, 2000. A great local field guide, although difficult to find. Lists Spanish names as well as medicinal/culinary uses of plants described and local folklore related to different species.

Oleg, Polunin and Smythies, *Flowers of Southwest Europe: A Field Guide*, Oxford University Press, 1998. Very comprehensive: this is a classic botanical must-have.

Ornithological Guides
Peterson, Mountfort and Hollom, *A Field Guide to the Birds of Britain and Europe*, Houghton Mifflin Company, 2001

Svensson, *Birds of Europe*, Princeton University Press, 2010

Svensson, Mullarney and Zetterstom, *Collins Bird Guide*, Collins, 2010

History and Travel

Ronda and Grazalema
Alastair Boyd, *The Road from Ronda*, Santana Books, 2014 (first published by Collins, 1969). An entertaining account of travels with a horse through the Ronda mountains.

Alastair Boyd, *The Sierras of the South*, HarperCollins, 1992. Wonderful anecdotes about life in the Ronda mountains.

Julian Pitt Rivers, *People of the Sierra*, University of Chicago Press, 1971. A fascinating anthropological study of the social structure of Grazalema in the 1950s.

Spain general
Gerald Brenan, *The Spanish Labyrinth*, Cambridge University Press, 2014. One of the best overviews of the conflict that ripped Spain apart in the late 1930s.

Antony Beever, *The Battle for Spain: The Spanish Civil War 1936–39*, Penguin Books, 2006

Richard Fletcher, *Moorish Spain*, University of California Press, 2006. An insightful account of an age that transformed Spanish culture and society.

John Gill, *Andalucía, A Cultural History*, Signal Books, 2008. A quirky and highly personal take on all things andaluz.

Walking – Trekking – Mountaineering – Climbing – Cycling

Over 40 years, Cicerone have built up an outstanding collection of over 300 guides, inspiring all sorts of amazing adventures.

 Every guide comes from extensive exploration and research by our expert authors, all with a passion for their subjects. They are frequently praised, endorsed and used by clubs, instructors and outdoor organisations.

All our titles can now be bought as **e-books**, **ePubs** and **Kindle** files and we also have an online magazine – **Cicerone Extra** – with features to help cyclists, climbers, walkers and trekkers choose their next adventure, at home or abroad.

Our website shows any **new information** we've had in since a book was published. Please do let us know if you find anything has changed, so that we can publish the latest details. On our **website** you'll also find great ideas and lots of detailed information about what's inside every guide and you can buy **individual routes** from many of them online.

It's easy to keep in touch with what's going on at Cicerone by getting our monthly **free e-newsletter**, which is full of offers, competitions, up-to-date information and topical articles. You can subscribe on our home page and also follow us on **Facebook** and **Twitter** or dip into our **blog**.

Cicerone – the very best guides for exploring the world.

CICERONE

Juniper House, Murley Moss, Oxenholme Road, Kendal, Cumbria LA9 7RL
Tel: 015395 62069 info@cicerone.co.uk
www.cicerone.co.uk and **www.cicerone-extra.com**